A GYPSY IN
AUSCHWITZ

A GYPSY IN AUSCHWITZ

Otto Rosenberg

as told to Ulrich Enzenberger

TRANSLATED BY HELMUT BÖGLER

LONDON
HOUSE

First published in Great Britain in 1999 by
LONDON HOUSE
114 New Cavendish Street
London W1M 7FD

A catalogue record for this book is available
from the British Library

ISBN 1 902809 02 5

Edited and designed by DAG Publications Ltd, London.
Printed and bound by Creative Print & Design Group Ltd,
Ebbw Vale, Gwent.

PUBLISHER'S NOTE
This book sets out to present as accurately as possible the idiom
and flavour of the original German text. In making the translation it
was felt that the language and style of the original spoken account
was far more authentic and convincing than would be the case were
the text to have been edited, rewritten or polished to make perfect
grammatical English. This is the way Otto Rosenberg told his
story – simply, as the memories came to him, and with
moving simplicity.

Contents

Introduction

This is the story of a human being. As the saying goes: a man like you or me. A Berliner born in 1927 recounts the story of his life. Born in Draugupönen, East Prussia, and raised in Germany's capital. National Socialism came to power, and only very few were able to escape it. He was one of the victims. Then came the war. When it finally ended, he was freed from the fear of death and mortal peril. A life could now start anew.

But the life that is being recounted here is not as normal as a cursory glance at the bare facts would make it appear. Because Otto Rosenberg did not fit into the norm prescribed in those days, a norm that continues to affect us to this day: he is a Sinto.* In this book a Sinto from Berlin tells the story of his life.

Today politics and the media in Germany are better able than ever before to deal sensibly with such terms as 'Sinti' and 'Roma'. But we Germans all know that we have not really succeeded in overcoming the traditional 'gypsy' image. Some things have actually changed since the Sinti and Roma first raised their voice in the late 1970s. They demanded to be

* Gypsies, mostly from France, Alsace and Germany, often travelling showmen and circus performers.

7

called what they had chosen to call themselves for centuries. With this they intended to break out of the old network of prejudices, simultaneously professing their independent tradition and conveying it to others.

Otto Rosenberg's childhood was poor, but somehow poverty was part of everyday life. The family was disciplined, partly from tradition, partly from deliberate choice. He was able to go to school, and he learned well and with enjoyment. Later there was even a sort of vocational training. But by then the course of events was being ever more harshly determined by National Socialism. One stage of forced labour led to the next. Hunger dominated the days, and fear the nights.

And then came Auschwitz. Otto Rosenberg does not present us with a general overview of this machine for the destruction of human beings. Nor does he provide a comprehensive statistic. He talks about himself and his neighbours, of the way they existed. His language is simple and sparse, it is – how else could it be – free of any embellishment. But in a most special way it conveys the horror of those days, the desperation, the fear.

Much has been written about Auschwitz, from varying points of view and with differing intentions. However, here speaks neither a Jew nor a Pole. This is the report of a Sinto. From his perspective we do not see the Holocaust in a new light, nor any less cruel. But we do see it from a different angle.

It is remarkable that amid all that horror, and in view of all that inhumanity, Otto Rosenberg still records those rare instances in which Germans helped him and his fellow sufferers. At the factory and in the camp, colleagues at work and guards. And his efforts to show the residue of humanity that still remained make it clear how terrible the times and how inhuman Germans in their numbers really were, many, many Germans: 'How what the SS and – as they say – Germans like you or me did was possible at all boggles the mind. That is something nobody can understand. Nobody knows why people can be like that.' And Otto Rosenberg sums things up: 'And I think there were very many German soldiers who were also good. But most of them were bad.'

Only now – more than fifty years later – did the author find the inner strength to recall things in such a way that he was able to write this book. It is not an indictment, it does not render account, nor does it call to account. A Sinto tells the story of his life. Today he lives in Berlin, just as normally as others in this city: a Berliner Sinto.

Klaus Schütz
Former Lord Mayor of Berlin
Berlin, February 1998

I

From the beginning, for as long as I can remember, and according to everything I had ever been told, we were German Sinti.[1]

My father traded in horses and my mother was a housewife. She went begging and told fortunes.

I was born in East Prussia, 1927, in Draugupönen. My parents had just split up, so I was then, two, three months old, taken to my grandmother in Berlin.

My granny said:

'Yes, the boy can stay with me.'

Later on my sister Therese followed, and then also my oldest brother Max, and the three of us all lived with our granny.

My second brother Waldemar was only with us for a little while and then went back to East Prussia to my father where my stepsister also lived, a daughter my father had by his first marriage. They stayed with father in East Prussia, in the area around Stallupönen and Gumbinnen, around Bialystok, all the way up to the Lithuanian border.

At about the age of five I again spent some time with my father, but not for long, only a few weeks. He was a very well-known man, even here in Berlin. He was about my size, in other words fairly small, but much heavier, weighed over 200 pounds and wore a goatee and twirled-up moustache. He played several instruments. There were many good things said about him, but because he also had a violent temper many people were afraid of him.

Many of our people travelled about in caravans. But my granny didn't care for this. We did move several times within Berlin, from Weißensee, Rennbahnstraße, Feldtmannstraße, Müllerstraße to Pankow-Heinersdorf and then to Alt-Glienicke. But we did not go on the road.

We lived simply and modestly on private lots we rented. Feldtmannstraße was fenced in on the street side and had a real gate. There were at least ten caravans there. When a place no longer suited us we hitched up. We borrowed the horses from relatives or friends. In the evening we still sat together around the fire, drank a bottle of beer and ate; and next morning, very early, we children heard the horses on the paved lot. We helped tighten the lines, put on the harnesses and then it was the caravan's turn. It normally had two door wings or a window in front that could be let down, and behind a covered wagon was hooked on in which the people who were helping us could ride back later. After we arrived the horses were unhitched. They got some chaff nicely kneaded through with feed and oats, and then a bundle of hay, and we first ate and then moved the wagons and set them up. We stayed and the others drove back again in the evening with their covered wagon. That was when they hung on a lantern, a paraffin lamp.

On the sides of the covered wagons there were iron bars or beams with slits in them to which slats and boards were fastened up to a height of about one and a half metres. Over this you put iron rods, or even better, freshly cut birch or hazelnut branches. These were bent, bound, and woven together, that was about as firm as anything. And over this came the canvas. To the right and left you built boxes, to sit on and to store stuff.

The horses were always very well tended. When a horse was to be traded or sold you needed smart boys to show it off. I did that several times. If the deal went through, there was halter money, ten or twenty pennies. If the horse lowered its head you had to joggle the harness until it looked up again nicely.

The women went begging and fortune-telling. The men wove baskets, made tables and chairs out of rootstock, and decorated cabinets. Later on all this was forbidden. Later on they had to do assigned work and were paid welfare money.

My mother's family was highly regarded among the Sinti. My grandmother's brothers were intelligent people, particularly my grand-uncle Anton and my grand-uncle Albert. They read books, were great at solving riddles, both wrote a very fine hand and had mastered spelling. They built Madonna chapels and decorated entire caravans with rootstock, just with an axe and a knife. They were the most versatile. Their brothers helped them, built scaffolds or whittled wooden nails.

The Rosenbergs conducted the negotiations with the authorities and were the ones you asked if you wanted to know something. My grandfather prepared documents. When someone died the brothers took care of the funeral arrangements and went round with a cap or hat and collected money. Then they took the money to a pub and drank it up. One of the brothers was good friends with the coffin-maker:

'Fit that out in such and such a way. When you're finished tell me how much it costs and I'll pay that.'

And that was the way it was. The money that had been drunk up, he paid it and the matter was closed. A sign that everybody helped one another.

Most of the people on the lot worked. They went serenading, and some tied on a pannier and sold haberdashery or leather goods. And then there were the lazybones, they did nothing, they sat in the corner and plunked their guitars. My uncle Florian, an immensely strong man, was a hod-carrier in the building trade. In those days there were no hoists. The bricks were loaded on a hod carried on the back, 150 pounds or more, and with this he climbed up three ladders.

There were also many card-games on the lot, Skat or Silesian lottery. We kids played a game with five stones. *Panschbara* is what we called it. We drew a grid in the sand with a stick and threw a chain into it. The young people did sports, lifted old wagon axles or played soccer. For a ball they stuffed their jackets into an old sweater and sewed it together.

It was particularly nice when there was a festival. Then several guitars got together, and violins and a bass, and also an accordion. There were always wonderful voices. My brother Max could sing marvellously. They always came for him when there was going to be a festival.

On the lots we were all just one big family. Everybody knew everybody. Total strangers never came in. We helped each other out with sugar and salt and onions, and if some of the women were still out, then the others made bread and butter for their children.

For me my parents were always more or less only visitors. When they came it was mostly late in the day, and I was already tired and fell asleep.

Once, I still remember, I was sitting with my mother in the caravan. She was cooking macaroni. I was sitting there on the bed waiting for the meal. And I went to sleep. When I woke up I was at my grandma's.

Later, afterwards, after the KZ* – before that I had never been able to talk with my mother about it – after the KZ I told her:

'Boy, you are some mother.'

Just for laughs.

'Do you remember, momma, when I was sitting with you in the caravan and you were cooking macaroni, and I went to sleep and didn't get any?'

'Oh', she said, 'my boy, I can still remember that. Yes, you had gone to sleep, but I gave them to your grandmother to take along. Such a big plateful! And I even said to her: you better take the macaroni along, otherwise he will claim later when he wakes up that he didn't get any.'

As a boy I was always hungry, and if somebody gave me something to eat I had to work very long and hard for it.

I was much closer to my grandmother than to my parents. Whenever she went somewhere she took me along. She was the one who taught me, and from her I learned what had taken place before my time.

Towards evening the fire would be lit and then the older women would gather round and tell many many stories from former times about relatives and people who had died. Or old fairy-tales, nicely invented stories, which sometimes could also be nasty. When she sat there my grandmother always

* Abbreviation for Konzentrationslager (concentration camp).

14

wrapped me in her apron and I could hear everything that was being told.

'Mammy!' I would say – I did not say grandmother, I said:

'Mammy, what was that? Were you there?'

'Yes, my boy.' Her voice was so soft and loving.

'Were you there too?'

'Oh, my boy, don't ask so many questions, I have a headache.'

And then I asked again:

'What is that, a headache? Mammy, tell me, what is it like when you have a headache?'

I always wanted to have a headache as a little boy, just to know what a headache was like. I never found out. Later on, of course, I did.

She never took any medicine, only 'Hoffmann's drops' when she felt sick. When she had a headache she put some vinegar on a cloth and tied it around her head. Or a rhubarb leaf. When the sun beat down my Mammy took a large rhubarb leaf, put it on her head and tied her shawl over it. This was a sort of protection from the sun.

We lived, in fact, very peacefully. It was in the days of Hindenburg. I can still remember the large five-mark pieces which showed his head.

We finally moved to Altglienicke-Bonsdorf, to Sandbacher Weg. It was probably my uncle Florian, the hod-carrier in construction, who had made this arrangement. We rented a flat there, a sort of superior garden hut, and a piece of land where we set up our caravan. By we I mean my granny, my brother Max, and also my brother Waldemar part-time, my sister Therese, uncle Florian, who also set up a caravan there, and his family, my young aunt Camba and her husband Paul, who was also still very young. There were also other people, among them a family called Krapp, a Bavarian who had married a Sintezza, with several children. They dealt in scrap, in screws and copper. And there we lived for several years.

We built ourselves wooden hutches for the chickens and rabbits, and we children kept the yard tidy and swept the street and picked up paper and cigarette butts. For this the owner sometimes gave us an ice cream or some sweets.

From Sandbacher Weg we then went to school.

Even then, already as a child, I was discriminated against, but as a child you see things differently. And I also defended myself. Against the children who were discriminating against me.

I always wore wooden clogs, I assume because there was no money for shoes. And with these wooden clogs I gained respect. They were very well suited for that.

The children wore their schoolbags strapped in front on their chests. And with these they played aeroplanes and bumped into me and called me names, that I was a dirty gypsy, and much more.

For this I once even beat up the son of a policeman with my clogs. Next day the policeman came into our classroom with his son. My heart nearly stood still out of fear. Our teacher, Mr Kühne, in my eyes a big man, about 1.80 to 2 metres tall, called me before the class and the policeman asked me several questions. Why had I done that?

I said:

'Because he insulted me, and because he shouted "dirty gypsy" behind my back. We got into a fight. He hit me and with his schoolbag he ... and then I took my clog and with the clog I then ...'

'Yes, that's enough.'

He talked to my teacher and I was allowed to go back to my seat. At first I thought the policeman was going to lock me up. As a child you have a special image of the police. But he didn't do it, and I was very glad about that. Later on my teacher took me to task: I should not do things like that, and if there was something wrong I should tell him and he would take care of it. And in general, after that they left me in peace.

One of my cousins, Oscar, also attended this Bonsdorf school. He also lived in Altglienicke. We two Rosenbergs sat on the same bench, and because there were hardly any school books we shared the same reader. When it was time to read we always read together and competed. I actually enjoyed that.

Christa Kühne, the daughter of teacher Kühne, was my girl-friend, and Gerda, Gerda Nitschke, was the girlfriend of Oscar, my cousin. Naturally we were not as well off as the daughters of the teachers. They could afford to drink milk and cocoa. Sometimes we were given Quaker buns, yes they were called Quaker buns, and milk, but only occasionally. The girls let us drink out of their milk or cocoa bottles by turning the straw around, and also gave us some of their breakfast. That was very nice.

One day I had a terrible experience. We were all sent to the showers and because my skin was a bit darker than that of my school-mates, they said:

'Come on, grab Otto and scrub him so that he becomes a little whiter.'

For them that was funny, but not for me. But my skin didn't come off and I still didn't become any whiter.

When school was out we often took a detour. Nearby, at Adlershof, there was a huge church, a convent, with nuns. When we came by an elderly nun, Sister Riecke, always said:

'God be with you, dear children, would you like a little soup?'

And we said:

'Yes'.

We then received a bowl of soup and a slice of bread. In times like those, even though we were still at peace, this was marvellous for us children. We always went by there, and then slowly made our way home..

The road workers who laid down asphalt and boiled tar fascinated me. I had to stop and watch and talk to them. Most times they gave me a piece of bread and butter and asked me what I did, where I came from, and I always gladly answered them.

And in back near the woods lived the Ingaschewski family, they were somehow connected with the church, we always prayed with them and were instructed in the faith. It was also very nice there.

Yes, that was long ago. We lived in peace.

My grandmother was a wonderful woman. She was so loving and good! She could get on with anybody, talk, and she took great care of us to make sure we were well off. We were not rich. We had the necessities. What you really need, that we had. And if our socks often had holes, and if she often sat there and mended stockings, or sewed a patch on a pair of trousers, or turned a shirt and a collar – we were always clean and decent, in other words not what you could call a dirty gypsy, not what would have confirmed such a prejudice.

I was always helpful, always in the expectation: if you do something, you will get something for it. And I always got something, even if it was only a sweet. But for me, that was also a form of recognition.

II

Then one morning, it could have been four or five in the morning, we were rousted out by SA and police.

Come on, get dressed! Quick, quick!'

Topsy-turvy. Our own policemen who we knew by sight were also there.

We were loaded onto a lorry. Our caravan was also taken along. We did not know where these people got the right to take us away from a private lot.

We were shipped to Berlin-Marzahn. Officially the place was called: Berlin-Marzahn Rastplatz. The Lot.

This was in 1936, before the Olympics.[2] I had just turned nine.

That was where we landed. In the beginning there was still tall grass there. When we children ran into it, we were gone. Then everything was mowed, dug up and levelled, and stones were laid where the water sources were. Afterwards it became a completely smooth lot.

They just unloaded us. We were detained. They said nobody is allowed to leave the lot.

There were ditches everywhere. The meadows around us were fields irrigated with sewage. And wagons constantly arrived and pumped sewage into the ditches. The smell was terrible. Normally we would never have stayed in such a place, if only because of our laws which forbid that. But we were forced to stay there.

Apart from that nobody showed any interest in us.

'It's up to you how you make out here.'

Today there are high-rises there. When I stand on the spot today, I can only find my bearings by the railway tracks, the fly-over, and the cemetery. The train passed right by the lot on the way to Werneuchen.

From the village of Marzahn you walked for about twenty minutes, then you came to our lot. Further on the road led to Falkenberg.

Well, there we were: my granny, my brother Max, my sister Therese, my fourteen- or fifteen-year-old aunt Camba, and I. Oscar was there too, also his father, my uncle Florian, my mother's brother; Bodo, Oscar's younger brother, his sister, and another brother, four siblings, just like us. The girl died later on in Marzahn. Jenny, yes she died later in Marzahn. More and more people kept arriving, and there was more and more sickness. The people then lived in huts knocked together out of sheet iron which they had to find for themselves if they wanted shelter. There was nothing there to be had.

A police barracks was set up, that yes. Next to the police barracks there was a school barracks because we were no longer allowed to attend the public school. That was the end for us.

The large school in Berlin-Marzahn, directly next to the village church, we were not allowed to attend. We only had one teacher. While there were several classes, there were only two rooms. One was for the very little ones. Some of the schoolbooks were free, but we also had to pay something. We had an exercise book for arithmetic, one for rough drafts, one for clean copies, a reader, and a maths book. We did not have anything more, that was it. We did not learn very much.

We were allowed to go shopping in the village. There was a milkman, Mr Drilling, a grocery store which also sold coal, that was Mr Haas, and we knew the blacksmith. We knew all the people there and they knew us. There was a stop next to the church, and that was the bus we always rode. We were allowed, after everybody had been given their papers and everything had been recorded, to leave the lot. We were also allowed to ride into the city, but we always had to return to the lot.

When we left we had to pass the police barracks. It had a huge window through which the whole lot could be observed. You had to walk right by the policemen. Mostly you also said hello to them, because you knew them, and when you came back as well. Other ways which would have been shorter for us when we went shopping or when we sometimes wanted to go to the station we were not allowed to use. Whoever trod on these ways had the dogs sicked on him, he was beaten up and probably also had to pay a fine.

But there were still people who managed to make things easier for themselves.

I can remember that when we needed fuel we had to walk on foot for up to twenty minutes. We could get coal from the dealer Willi Haas, in sacks weighing 50 or 25 pounds. I hoisted the sack on my shoulder and on the way back I rested time and again. I was a boy of nine, ten years.

Fetching water, fetching wood, fetching coal – I did a lot on foot. Sometimes I walked three, four times a day from the lot to the village church in Marzahn. The woman at the baker's always said:

'Now, deary, what is it going to be today? Did you forget to wash your eyes again?'

Later a certain Fuhrmann sold milk on the lot, and Walter Schwarz opened a general store there. He did good business.

In the icy winter I went to fetch milk, half an hour on foot. My hands were like hooks. Sometimes I was even sorry for myself. It always hurt my granny very much. It often made her scold people, particularly when they said I had done something wrong. She would ask me:

'Tell me, did you do that?'

'No Mammy, it was not me.'

I never lied to my granny, never, never, never. Why? Because she was the person I loved best, and then you always tell the truth. My granny would then get up and say:

'It was not my son, and I know that if it had been my son he would have told me.'

If I had really had done something I said:

'Yes, that was me.'

And then she said:

'Come on, get inside here!'

But so commanding. Then she took a carpet-beater or a slipper, hit it against something and said:

'Go on, scream!'

And I would always go:

'Ouch! Ouch! Ouch!'

The people outside thought: now she is beating him. But she did not punish me. No, no.

Once some Turkish Sinti came with a small circus with horses. They also had several monkeys with which they went begging, trained monkeys who then passed the hat around, and brown bears who danced to the tambourine. I had a Turkish girlfriend. Her name was Katharina and she sometimes gave me a few pennies.

Once a monkey got me. I wanted to go and see her and passed very close to the cage. Although he was on a chain, I was so close that he was able to grab me by the head. He pushed me down, began to look for lice, and did not want to let go again. There was nothing left for me to do but to call for help:

'Katharina! Katharina!'

She only spoke Turkish. The monkey knew how to jump backwards, somersault, he was able to do all that.

The daughter of my granny's brother married a Turkish Sinti at the time.

My brother Max once brought me an old Prussian spiked helmet. I polished it until the scales shone. In those days I played a lot with the son of a Roma family who was my age. He had a little dog. And one day this little boy appeared in a military uniform, with a helmet and Swastika and combat belt and a sabre, the whole works. I thought that was lovely, I would have liked to have that too.

At Christmas everybody always tried to make something so as to offer a present to somebody else, to bring joy.

Once a bishop came to the lot, in the evening, it was already dark, with a donkey and a midget. He had a real bishop's hat on and a big staff in his hand and went around, to the children. The donkey was carrying a satchel, and every child got a bag with an apple and some sweets. The bishop greeted every child and laid on his hand. He came to me too. For me this was something great, gigantic. I was still quite small for my age.

I looked sort of like this and hesitatingly gave him my hand. It was so soft and – yes, really pleasant and was in a huge glove and was as soft as angora. That caused me great joy. And then I also got a bag – another, even greater joy.

Lots of people who were curious came by who took photographs and sometimes even sneaked onto the lot. Then the police came and immediately chased them away:

'Get off!'

But the Catholic sisters and missionaries always found a way. They came from Strausberger Platz among other places, from the Christ-the-King-House. Although there was no Mass said in Marzahn, songs of God were sung and pictures of Jesus explained. That was a lovely thing, but you also have to mention that the Catholic and Evangelic churches handed over the parish registers and thereby supported the persecution of the Sinti and Roma.

We children regularly visited the Christ-the-King-House. There we were instructed in the catechism, every Friday evening, after school. We could stay there overnight too. On Sunday we rode back home. We were given food and slept in a dormitory.

There were Father Petrus, Brother Williges, and Brother Boniface. The last had a huge hump. But they were all very nice. Director Trüding instructed us in the catechism, in the Catholic faith, until we went to Communion.

For the first Holy Communion they made clothes for us. We were given high-heeled wooden shoes and suits with a white detachable collar. At Christ-the-King-House we were happy. The food tasted so good, and in the afternoon or for supper there was always a tasty sweet soup in a big cup, in a mug, and with this baked or fried dumplings. I can still remember the taste of them, but have never eaten them again since, was never again given them. The food alone attracted us to go there.

And then they said: if you want to stay here, after all, the times are bad, then it would be nice if Otto were to become a server. We had already begun to learn a bit of Latin, the prayer on the altar steps.

'Et introibo ad altarem dei...'

I was already all set to go. If things had gone on as before I would probably have stayed in this Christ-the-King-House, and with my way of thinking and looking at things, and because of my faith, if the war had not intervened, maybe have become a priest. But that is something you just can't tell.

The anthropologist Dr Ritter and Eva Justin also came to the lot.[3] The two of them went systematically from barracks to barracks and from caravan to caravan and went straight to the point. They gave people a bag of coffee:

'Why don't you first make a nice cup of coffee!'

They questioned the people about their origins, where they came from, their parents, about their mother, about the grand-parents and so on. Now some were able to give information, but some who were older didn't have everything at their fingertips. I remember a big, strong old woman of at least eighty whose hair they cut off because of this. Terrible, if you really think about it. Maybe she had not told the truth, or not what Justin and Dr Ritter wanted to hear, and had run away and had hidden herself at Falkenberger Weg. The two of them had run her to earth there with the help of the police and brought her back. Then they cut off her hair. Just imagine, such an old woman! Then all she had on her head were these bristles! It was already cold, and then they even poured ice-cold water over her and she had to stand still on the spot and was, I believe, dead within three days. Those are the kind of things they did! I did not see it happen, but I saw the woman when she was dead, and saw her white prickly hair. She was not buried in a coffin but in a sort of tin box in the Marzahn cemetery.

There are still a number of graves there of Sinti and Roma who died in those days, including the grave of little Jenny. But many graves were also levelled in and in their place you can now only see the Sinti stone which we put up and where we always meet on the second Sunday in June.

Eva Justin and Dr Ritter also came to our family:

'When? Where? Where? Where?'

Yes. What we knew we told them.

They investigated everywhere, at school too. On this occasion Eva Justin said:

'I would like to have Otto come to me after school at the Institute for Anthropology.'

So I then rode to this institute.

'Well, then sit down. Oh look, here we have such a lot of beads, why don't you just take them!'

In front of me there was a piece of wire with a thread attached to it.

I began to thread various beads.

'Let me see! Oh, beautiful!'

She wrote everything down. Then she gave me a game of skill, a board with holes around which you had to manoeuvre a little ball. And showed me pictures: children running away, a broken pane, a man coming out, catching one. I still remember that one exactly. I was supposed to explain what was happening. And I did too.

She took me off on a bicycle, on the carrier. We rode along Unter den Eichen and over a bridge. In Curtiusstraße, that is where she had a house, a corner house, and her mother also lived there.

I was given a room and a little bed, how should I describe it, to me it was an angel's bed. I was allowed to sleep there. And I was given food and drink. That was fantastic. And she was also very friendly and very nice and very kind to me.

It was only afterwards I realized that she had simply done a test on me. Of course I didn't find that to be quite as good. It would have been better if I had been given a beating. I could have stood that better than this. I still ask myself today: how could she do something like that when she was so nice and kind? This makes me feel worse than any punishment would have.

I then worked at the institute for a longer period. Worked satisfactorily. I pasted slides together. Once or twice a week. I did not get any money. Probably my fare, but I'm no longer sure.

Eva Justin's mother was a fantastic woman. She was a wonderful cook and as a boy this counted for a lot. She gave me kohlrabi. I remember that as if it were yesterday. I was used to kohlrabi raw, but I had never eaten them cooked. And since they were woody I didn't eat them.

'Very well, if you do not eat them now, you will eat them later or tomorrow.'

Next day they were served to me again. I had to eat them then because I was not given anything else. But there was a bottle of Maggi sauce on the table and so I seasoned the kohlrabi.

'You see, it works after all, doesn't it?'

When somebody is so good and nice to you, and later on you learn that she only did this because ... that boggles my mind.

I have no other explanation except that she did not like me as much as she pretended to. Maybe she did like me a bit but was also doing her job at the same time. I don't know. I did not speak to her again after the war, even though she continued to practise in Frankfurt with Dr Ritter.

I personally could not have painted a negative picture of her. How come? If a person is good, then you can't say anything bad about her.

One evening I had the horrors about sleeping in that room in her house.

'What of?'

'Something unknown', I said. It was probably ghosts.

And then at the institute, those monkey skulls and skeletons in the glass cabinets! I did not want to go inside into those rooms. And she locked me in there. For half an hour, or an hour, I don't remember any more. I cried and was afraid, and also angry of course. Maybe it was not for as long as all that, but for me it seemed very long. Then she opened up again.

'Well, are you still afraid? You saw that they can't harm you. You do not need to be afraid of them.'

Maybe she wanted to take away my fear, but even so I was still afraid.

III

In 1938 the police came again, or the SA – I no longer recall
exactly – and collected all the young men and drove them away
in lorries to Sachsenhausen, Oranienburg.[4] Among others my
uncle Paul, the husband of my mother's sister.

From there many of them were sent to other camps. Some
came back to Marzahn. But most did not.

My uncle had had to slice bread in Sachsenhausen and
came back with a bad injury, with a bandaged hand.

'I am not allowed to say a single word,' he said. 'If I tell
anything here they will come and take me again.'

Then he did begin to tell, in bits and pieces, what had gone
on in Sachsenhausen. That sure did make you afraid. And
then, from time to time, the threats began:

'If you do not behave yourself here then you will be put
into the concert-camp!'

Yes, concert-camp was what they said. That sounds fine,
doesn't it.

In the meantime barracks had been brought in and foun-
dations laid and the barracks set up. These were former army
barracks. They were partitioned in the middle and were occupied on both sides, one family each side. We were given
barrack 28a.

There was my grandmother, my grand-uncle Anton, my young aunt Camba, my brother Max, my sister, and I.

I rarely had a fight with my sister, only some bickering now and again. And the same was true for our whole community. With us there was no beating. Only from our other relatives if at all, but they should rather have beaten their own children, not us. Because I was growing up with my grandmother, without a father and a mother, everybody thought they could order me about.

Behind the police barracks an infirmary room was built for women who were having babies. The women stayed in this infirmary building until they were able to come back to us.

Next to this infirmary building there was a second room, the welfare office. That is where people went who did not have any job, like for example old uncle Pipper, who had formerly always gone serenading with his zither. I still remember that he never wanted to ride on the bus. He always said:

'I won't ride on a devil's contraption like that, I won't get on.'

My granny also went to the welfare office, like most of the older women. She received I don't know how much, but in any case a few marks per month.

There was a certain Mr Huckauf there, he was a moral coward. And a Mr Schukalla. He had a red face, played the strong man and was happy that everybody was afraid of him. One day he took me out of school and drove with me to Lichtenberg. There he bought me a pair of knickerbockers, one of those knee-length trousers, and new shoes and a cap to go with them. The idea was to do something good for us. I looked like new. Neat. You can imagine how proud I was to go to school like that.

31

He barked like a dog. My uncle met him again after the war. And Mr Schukalla said to him:

Well, it wasn't all that bad in Marzahn, was it. We gave you a few knocks on the head, huh, but that was all.'

I do not know how it came about, but in the school on the lot I became a prefect, and my sister too, me for the boys and she for the girls. Maybe it was because we tried very hard, to work, to help where we could.

I had a very close relationship with my sister Therese. After all, we were the youngest of us brothers and sisters. She had a defective heart valve. When her heart was not beating correctly her head shook, that is how serious it was. In those days, I have to say this, we were too stupid to take her to a hospital. She had some drops prescribed, but they didn't help any. I cannot judge how hard it was for her to do the work she had to do as a girl: cleaning, washing the dishes, sweeping out the caravan.

In the morning I was always the first in school. I was allowed to ring a big bell that hung on a rope in front of the door.

'Ding, ding, ding...'

That was to bring the children out of their barracks or caravans.

The cleaning woman had already tidied up. Then the teacher came and stood in front. The German greeting:

'Heil Hitler! Sit!'

Then the first thing was:

'Hands on the desk!'

Whoever had dirty fingernails or dirty fingers was sent out to wash. Then he was allowed back in.

When there were breaks in between, it was:

'Take off your shoes! Show your feet!'

Whoever had dirty feet had to go wash them.

I found that very funny. That was quite all right. Outside there was the pump. Somebody had to pump and the others washed themselves and ran around. For children that is nice.

When pupils were missing the teacher said to me:

'Otto, go and tell them they should come to school.'

I went and knocked on the door of the caravan or barracks. Sometimes they were still in bed, were completely dishevelled, and had feathers in their hair.

'Man, you have to come to school, the teacher is waiting!'

'Oh, we overslept!'

Then they got ready in a hurry and came. The teacher, Mr Barwich, would scold, but then he would calm down again.

I got along well with everybody, with the police too, with leading constable Politz. With chief constable Bredel too. People were afraid of him, but I was not afraid. They all knew me.

'Otto, come here, go fetch some coal from the shed!'

'Otto, fetch some water!'

I never said no, not even once. And what did it get me in the end? They gave me something and even seemed to like me.

A trustie took care that the lot was kept clean. He fixed numbers to the barracks, and on the caravans too, so that anybody could be found immediately. When people came in at night he wrote down their names in order to report them to the police.

Time and again visitors came who walked around on the lot accompanied by the police and looked at everything and discussed it.

Soon about 900 to 1000 people lived in the Marzahn camp, not only Sinti, but also lots of Roma.

Among the Sinti there were many uncles and aunts of mine, but also other relatives, like for example the sister of my granny and her sons. We were a huge family.

One of the brothers of my grandmother had the same name as me, Otto. One day I received a package from the Christ-the-King-House with toothpaste, toothbrushes, handkerchiefs. I was still waiting for the postman while my uncle Otto had already collected the package.

'Tell me, do you have a package for Otto Rosenberg?'

'Yes, I delivered the package at such and such a place.'

I went to my grand-uncle and said:

'That is my package.'

'Now then boy! My name is on it.'

'All right, but in the package there is...'

'All right, fine, then...'

There must have been at least fifty of us in the family. And these people worked.

My uncle Florian continued to work as a hod-carrier. He bought nice things for himself, including a leather waistcoat. In those days that was something real special.

One of them worked in Neukölln in a wax factory, like so many, one for Hasse and Frede, that was a stone mill, and another in a crate factory in Hohenschönhausen.

My brother Max who had worked in the 'Cabaret of Comedians' here in Berlin, was drafted into the North German Ball-bearing Factory in Neu-Lichtenberg. He was also even mustered into the army and classed as replacement reserve two. He had a German girlfriend. That was not permitted because of 'impurity of blood'.[5] And so he was sent into the KZ Neuengamme and towards the end of the war he was on one of those ships the British bombed by mistake. He tried to save himself and was shot.

Only the older people stayed on the lot and the children went to school. The system was almost, but not quite completely, organized. Everybody knew where everybody else was. Everybody was registered. Whoever was able went to work.

On Saturdays and Sundays things looked bad as far as bread was concerned, there was no more bread left. My granny had many more children and grandchildren, and they were no better off than we were. And then they came round and demanded bread and got it too. Sometimes I was angry about this and said:

'Now they are going to eat it all up! And then I will have nothing left for me!'

I can remember that I cried.

'Why has God singled me out to heap such misfortune on me that I am always hungry!'

I cried because I had nothing to eat. My granny was only given welfare support. We didn't do any big business deals.

I worked for the farmer on the other side of the railway tracks. Apples, pears, plums, and potatoes, I got them all there. I had the run of the farm. I took the cow to pasture and cleaned up. They were not afraid that I would take something or abuse their confidence.

'Otto, you can go and pick cherries today.'

I picked maybe five baskets full, or more, and for that I was given one.

'You can take that one along for your granny.'

I also helped out with other farmers, during the beet harvest. For one row I got seventy-five pennies and two Belgian buns with icing. Sometimes we were given less money and instead plenty to eat. Coffee with lots of milk, that was something we could not afford at home. We were glad that we had enough to eat, and could still take fifty or seventy-five pennies home to granny. In those days that was a lot of money. A roll cost two or three pennies, a bun with crumble topping a *sechser*, in other words five pennies. For three or four marks you could cook a beautiful meal for everybody.

The grown-ups also worked on the farms a lot. Some of the farmers had huge beet fields. If you began with the beet-pulling very early in the morning you only finished your row by nine or ten o'clock. We children never made it. For a row as long as that the grown-ups received several marks. By evening they had sometimes made six, seven marks. On top of that came the pennies from the kids, that made ten or fifteen marks in all. That was enough to live off for a whole week.

I was a well-known figure, everywhere, whether at Father Philipp or at Rhode, that was a big farmer and a Nazi. Already in those days he drove a Mercedes, a green Mercedes.

I often sat in front of the big Marzahn church at the bus stop. I waited for acquaintances or just looked to see who came. And all the while I looked at the portal of the church and dreamed about the exchange thaler the old people talked about.

To get hold of this thaler you have to find a cat, put it in a sack and tie this sack with ninety-nine knots. With this you go to the church at midnight and draw a circle in front of the portal of the church with chalk, stand inside it and wait until the bell strikes twelve. Then you wave the sack and say:

'I have a lovely rabbit for sale.'

It doesn't take long before the devil appears and says:

'Yes, I would like to buy that rabbit.'

'Yes.'

'How much does the rabbit cost?'

'One thaler.'

'Only one thaler?'

'Yes, only one thaler. I will give you the rabbit, and you give me one thaler.'

'Done.'

Then you give him the sack, and the devil quickly undoes the ninety-nine knots. That takes a while. Then he looks into the sack and sees that he has been cheated. He immediately rips the cat to pieces and wants to grab you, but he can't get at you because you are standing inside the chalk circle. Now he tries every way he knows to get you to come out. You have to stand firm until the clock strikes one.

'Gong, gong!'

Then the devil is gone. But you have to stay inside your circle and sit down until it gets light. And then you will see a thaler on the ground, and you can spend it as often as you like. It will always return to your pocket.

As a child I firmly believed in this fairy-tale. And so I sat on a bench in front of the church in Marzahn, at the bus stop, and dreamt about the exchange thaler.

In the bus we Sinti were not permitted to sit downstairs on the upholstered seats, we had to go upstairs onto the hard wood.

The threats became stronger and stronger. You did notice that the police were a little different, everything had become stricter and tighter.[6]

If somebody had done something, or if in the evening or at night there were arguments on the lot, or fights, the police put on a gigantic spotlight and ran into the blinding light with drawn sabres – they had those long sabres and not yet the short army sabres – just like you sometimes see in the movies. Like cops and robbers, that is about how it seemed to me. I saw that with the eyes of a boy, but I also saw that people were beaten with those sabres. Not with the sharp edge but with the flat side. Then the riot squad came, and the people were seized, and up on the wagon and taken away.

Before then, if there was conflict on a lot you left and went to look for another. That was now no longer possible. The people in Marzahn were of different descent and backgrounds. One person came from Hungary, another from Austria, yet another was German. And so there were often disagreements, mostly because of the children. The grown-ups seldom quarrelled. They knew: we all have to hang together. But when the children fought among themselves, and one of them made the other bleed, then one word led to the next, and then the women set about it. The men went in to try to separate them, and then something else went wrong and before you knew it half the lot was in an uproar. And then your 'friend and helper' came and calmed things down and took many away and locked them up.

And soon more and more people were taken away, and then you could already hear: you will get a piece of land and can settle in the East. Those are the sorts of slogans that ran through the – KZ is what you could call it by then, yes.

Our teacher, who now also appeared in uniform, showed us on the map where our German troops were, where they were marching in. We followed all that.

From time to time he liked to take a little swig. He wrote a problem on the board and then withdrew into his room.

'Otto, make sure that they keep quiet and write!'

When the husband of the farmer who lived directly opposite was drafted, our teacher became friendly with her. They were not big farmers. They only had one cow, it was called Minka. But there were probably good things to eat.

One day our teacher gave me a letter and I thought I was supposed to take it to the big school in Marzahn. I ran, that was a stretch of twenty, twenty-five minutes. When I came back the teacher asked me:

'What kept you so long? Did you deliver the letter?'

'Yes, to the director.'

I was supposed to have taken it to the farm lady! I ran back again to Marzahn.

'Excuse me, Mr Director, but the letter was not meant for you.'

'I have already noticed that.'

Well, our teacher was angry, but there was not much he could do about it.

In the meantime there were frequent air-raid warnings. There were no bunkers for us, and if we happened to be in the city we were not allowed into the public air-raid shelters. In the camp at Marzahn we left the caravans and barracks and watched the spectacle. We children found it quite interesting

39

the way the searchlights of the flak chased the bombers. But often splinters from the shells of the air defence flew into the camp, then we had to watch out. They were as sharp as knives. The next day we children always collected them.

There was a flak position near by. I often visited the soldiers there. As soon as I appeared they said:

'Come here, Otto, you are probably hungry again.'

Once they were cooking lovely fat yellow peas. It must have been a Catholic holiday. My granny was asleep on the sofa and I woke her up:

'Look here Mammy, I have brought you something real nice.'

Then she remembered that it was a holiday.

'Oh, my boy, today I was not allowed that.'

'Oh Mammy, you have eaten some already. Now it no longer matters.'

I must admit, I admired those soldiers, those big, blond, blue-eyed men in their pretty uniforms.

At this time no stranger was allowed on the lot any longer. Our police were now posted directly at the front gate. In the morning they would come to a given barracks or to given caravan and take the people away never to be seen again.

More and more people were being ordered to report to Alexanderplatz, Dircksenstraße, Berlin C Two, to the office for gypsies, to Karsten.[7]

This was the man who had total authority.

Among others my mother was told to report there. By now she was also in Marzahn. She too had to go to Dircksenstraße and did not come back either. She was sent straight to Ravensbrück.

I can remember that I waited at the village church for the last bus on which she was supposed to come, and then she did not come again. I hardly dared to go home, because it was so dark, so lonely, but I had to go home after all.

And that is how they took away many people singly.

IV

At the age of thirteen I was discharged from school, and because my granny was on welfare and I was now already a big boy I was expected to support her.[8]

I had to go to the employment office, was given a work-book, tax card, and social security card, and was drafted into a company making arms. It was called Dannemann und Quandt Apparatebau, Berlin-Lichtenberg, but was an armaments firm making shells for submarines. I was very popular with my foreman and with my colleagues at work.

I worked as a helper in the spray paint shop and suggested an improvement in the dipping process. For varnishing they always only took one ring and dipped it. You pulled each indi-vidual ring off an iron rod, hung it on a hook, dipped it in, took it out again, hung it up to dry, and then threaded it back on the rod. For me that was too slow.

So I said to Mr Levin – today I assume that he was Jewish: 'I need a long tub.'

Levin had done welding and soldering. He was a jack-of-all-trades. In the shop he knew everything.

He welded a long tub for me.

Then I said to the foreman:

'I need a big tub full of paint, not a little bit like this.'

I poured the paint into the long tub. Then I threaded the rings onto the iron rod in a dry condition, dipped them in, let them drip off and hung them into the cart for the baking.

They had been paying me thirty-one pennies an hour, and because of this dipping process I was paid four pennies more an hour, in other words, I got thirty-five pennies an hour.

You can imagine how I felt. I was jubilant. But within only a very short time it all changed completely.

The foreman came to me and said:

'Otto, I can no longer approve the heavy duty work card for you.'

'And why not? I work here in the spray paint shop, and because of the paint...'

'No.'

The milk – we were all entitled to milk – I was also no longer permitted to have. Orders from upstairs.

'Why? What about the others?'

No milk. And the few grams of extra meat that were on the heavy duty work card I no longer received either.[9]

Next I was excluded from the community meal at lunchtime. That was the most terrible thing. Can you imagine something like that? I had not harmed anybody and was still a child in my thoughts and my actions. I was also no longer allowed to sit at the breakfast table where all my colleagues were having breakfast. I was no longer permitted to take part. I had to eat my bread outside on a timber pile in the yard. I was no longer allowed to sit at the table.

Now I really did feel backed into a corner and put down. Many people were sorry about this. They passed me something on the sly and encouraged me. But there were also many others whom this did not bother at all.

Mr Fisher, one of the original members of the company, about one-sixty tall, with a twirled-up moustache, filled my lunch into a mess-tin and placed it next to the woodpile.

'There is nothing else I can do, Otto.'

He put my lunch down for me. And he was not allowed to do that.

Many people then no longer talked to me or greeted me.

At Christmas time a certain Knop packed up some children's things for me and said:

'Boy, take that along with you.'

Maybe many would have liked to be nicer to me, but they were afraid of the Gestapo, that people would say:

'He is giving things to the gypsy.'

That they might then be ordered to report.

The foreman – he wore a black uniform with a Swastika but was not SS – what this uniform meant I don't know – the foreman Günther called me to him:

'Rosenberg!'

But really commanding, like that.

I entered his office.

'Take that, but tuck it away so that nobody will see it.'

And he gave me a glass of jam.

Afterwards when he came and I was at work, he made a big show about how strict he was to me. But he wasn't.

'Come on. come on, the broom, whisk, whisk, whisk, whisk!'

But he was OK. I went to see him after 1945. By that time he was working for a different company. I greeted him and also thanked him.

The daily way to work was the worst for me. Actually you had to make a big detour so as not to pass the police, but I usually walked along the tracks, direction Lichtenberg. The train stopped at Marzahn. It did not only consist of passenger cars, so I often jumped onto a freight car and hid in the brakeman's cab. In the summer that was great, but in winter! If you went past the police to the bus, and it had snowed, then it often did not run. Then you had to go back almost the whole way to the station, and then the train was often already gone, and the next one only left half an hour later. And when you walked along the railway tracks and it was icy and you slipped, then you slid down the high embankment almost into the wires.

'Ding. ding, ding, ding.'

If anyone was caught, the police had him bitten by dogs, he was beaten, and then also summoned. That never happened to me, thank God.

So sometimes I arrived one or two hours late. Then the chief foreman Kramer always came round – by the way I also saw him again after 1945, but as soon as he recognized me he was gone in a flash – and said:

'Well Rosenberg, if you are late again then you know you will be sent to the KZ.'

Every time. If you hear this time and again, if you are regularly censured for the same offence, and if this keeps happening even though you have no bad intent, then one day you get fed up.

Finally I said to him:

'Go get stuffed.'

I was still a lad. He should have tried to put himself in my place. Work started at seven, that meant I had to get up at four-thirty, and I was a boy of fifteen. The way he was already waiting for me ... and then the way he talked down at me, so superior:

'Well, well, Rosenberg! Late again. Well, well. Note that down. Just keep on like this. You'll wind up in the concert-camp.'

Despite this I was still the gofer. I went for lemonade, beer and also for cigarettes, and if somebody was missing I went for his cigarettes too and gave them – I didn't smoke – to somebody else, and from him I then got something to eat.

The kiosk where I had to shop was in the army hall. That was where the finished submarine shells lay.

One day I was passing through the hall again and saw a 'magnifying glass'. It was probably used to examine the shells for faults and cracks, but at the time I did not know this.

Wow, I thought, this really enlarges terrifically.

I unscrewed it and with it I burned some letters, the way boys do, into the stack of wood where I ate – they could have checked this later on. Yes, and somebody must have seen me. In any case Siebert, this was a colleague, came:

'You, Otto, the chief foreman Kramer saw you. You unscrewed the lens or magnifying ...' – I don't recall whether he said magnifying glass or lens – from there.'

In my sudden panic I lifted up the paint kettle and shoved the thing underneath it.

'I didn't unscrew anything there'.

'Yes you did,' he said, 'don't do anything stupid. Foreman Schmäler saw you, and Kramer too. Give it back and they will screw it back on and the whole thing will be over.'

I said: 'Yes, right: I didn't want to take it away, all I wanted was to...'

So I gave him the glass. They screwed it back on, and every-thing seemed to have been taken care of.

It was four o'clock. Work was over for me and I was leaving the plant. The guard at the gate told to me to come in and sit down.

'What for?' I asked. 'What am I supposed to do here?'

'Well, just wait.'

I waited for a while.

The door opened and a policeman came in.

'Is that him?'

'Yes', said the guard, 'that's him.'

'Don't you want to stand up!'

A tone, such a tone, really! I did not know what to make of it. He put a line on me, a choke chain, around my arm, took me to the tram and rode with me to some police station. Embarrassing this was for me, terrible!

There they wrote everything down about the glass, and I was arrested. They wanted to lock me into a cell.

'Do not lock me in, leave the door open!'

They left the door open and gave me a pail and a rag.

'You have nothing better to do anyway, you can wipe up the floor.'

When I was finished it was probably at least six or seven.

'I have been at work since early this morning. I am hungry.'

One of them said:

'I still have some bread.'

And another policeman:

'Well I still have some jam.'

So they gave me something and I ate.

Then they wanted to lock me into the cell again!

'No, I won't go in there', I said. 'At least leave the door open!'

I had never been in there before. You become scared, don't you?

They left the door open after all.

In the morning I was taken to Dircksenstraße.

I was taken down to the cellar, to the men. Lots of unkempt men, at least thirty, forty men. No beds, no chairs, no room, just a small table and hordes of cockroaches. And there you are, shoved in, door closed, finished, over. I said to myself:

For God's sake, where have you landed up!

There was no toilet either, just a curtain behind which there were tubs and that – uuuugh...

What should I do? There was no place to sleep. I crawled under the table and pulled – I was still wearing my coat – it over my head. And so I went to sleep.

The next morning the door opened, and suddenly I heard:

'Otto Rosenberg!'

'Here!'

Oh, I thought, thank God you are going to be set free!

The end of the tale: I was put on a transport to Moabit, Berlin 12a, in handcuffs. Through the gate, out you get and inside. First I had to wait, in a cell. Then step forward. What I was wearing I was allowed to keep. Everything else they took away. My papers too. As a boy you don't have very much – a few buttons or a few pennies in your pocket.

Then off to the house-father, that was what he was called. That's where you got chequered bedding, a pillowcase and so forth. Then upstairs. And already I heard:

'F5, a new admission!'

But how that resounded! You just have to try to imagine! How old was I at the time? Fifteen, sixteen?

I was taken upstairs to the cell, into cell 538. Inside, door slammed behind me. I thought the sky would fall in. A solitary cell!

About half an hour later I had to come out again, for a shower.

A machine was positioned on the centre of my head and I was shorn bald.

After the shower I was given a pair of prison trousers and a jacket and a scarf. I was allowed to keep my coat and shoes.

It was clean. I was glad to have got out of Dircksenstraße. In the beginning I didn't know anything at all about what the rules were.

I then spent four months in that cell in solitary, without a trial, without anything.

You had to wear the prison scarf all the time. The scarf had to be looped around the neck in a certain way and the end pulled through. Once the chief guard grabbed me, reached into the space between neck and scarf and strangled me until I was out of breath. All I had done was to ask somebody whether he had had any sausage. I hadn't received any. The trusties regularly misappropriated part of the food.

Everything was under strict control. When the guard opened the cell door for the first time, I was naturally standing in the middle of the cell.

'Why aren't you standing under the window? Get under the window immediately! Stand at attention and report your cell!'

How was I supposed to know that? When the door was unlocked you had to go back under the window immediately.

Nobody had told me anything about that. I asked:

'What am I supposed to report?'

He told me:

'Cell 538, occupied by one prisoner awaiting trial. Nothing to report.'

My young aunt Camba came to see me and brought me shoes. She told me that by far the largest part of our family had been shipped out of Marzahn.[10]

Finally a date was set. I had been assigned a lawyer, but he was on the side of the court, not on my side. Probably a Nazi too.

I was sentenced to three months and three weeks in a community home for sabotage, yes, and theft of military equipment, yes. But I had already done four months.

I was then let go, I had already done my time. I was still hardly out when other police came, nobody from the prison police, and they arrested me again.

'You are under arrest.'

I asked:

'Why? I have just been released from this prison here! I am free!'

'Inspection.'

And so I was taken back to Dircksenstraße to Karsten, the one I mentioned earlier, to the gypsy office. There was a Sinto sitting with him who lived in Marzahn with his family in a caravan and reported everything to Karsten. And Karsten said:

'Four months? That was quite a long time.'

And this man said, but really cynically:

'Well, how was it? Was it nice?'

I answered: 'Yes, it was nice.' That was all I could say.

Then Karsten said to him:

'Well what are we going to do with him?' And to me:

'What are we going to do with you now? Where are we going to put you?'

'With my aunt,' I said. I knew that there was almost nobody left in Marzahn. And then this man said:

'He is going where his father and mother are.'

I did not know what that meant. So I was real happy about this.

After the war some Sinti handed this man over to the Russians. The Russians said:

'Why don't you just knock him over the head! You can kill him, nothing will happen to you.'

But in the end they didn't do that. One of our women beat him about the ears with something. With us this is one of the worst possible insults. The traitor was then sent to Siberia.

At first I was again put into a cellar vault. There I saw three families with small children. I was satisfied because before I had always been alone.

Later a girl also came in. The others joked:

'She can't sleep with us. She has to sleep with you.'

But she did not sleep with me, she slept at my feet. I lay this way and she lay that way.

But it was also unpleasant – no real toilet and so forth, the most unpleasant thing you can imagine. We waited for a few weeks. Then the shipment left.

This is when I was separated from these families.

I no longer recall from where the train departed.

I still counted as a prisoner, as an arrestee, and was put into a special car. This car was full of children, finely dressed, with bread bags and cases. Sinti children, Roma children, I don't know. Some of them didn't look like Sinti or Roma at all. They came from homes, Catholic homes. Sweet faces. In any case, they were all six, eight years old. The whole car was full of them.

The police took me and stuck me in a cell in front at the entrance and locked me in there. There was a sort of a seat inside, and I sat there.

The police left and then the military took over the shipment, I think. The guard sat there stiffly with his carbine and did not let anybody near me.

After we had been riding along for a while, the children began to ask the Red Cross nurse who was accompanying them why I was locked in. She said to the guard:

'Why don't you let the boy out? There is no place he can go! Where do think he could go?'

He let me out and I went to sit with the children. They all had full bread tins and bread bags.

'I am hungry, I haven't eaten anything.'

Then they gave me some of their meal.

And so shortly before my sixteenth birthday I arrived in Auschwitz by train.

But I did not meet father or mother there.

V

In Groß-Auschwitz, in big Auschwitz right out in front, that is where the reception took place. The train had been put together out of several shipments and the sorting out began immediately. The Jews over there, the Sinti over there, the Poles over there and so forth. Everything was organized. You were taken to a doctor. He gave a signal, mostly with a bell, and made a gesture. That way, that way, that way. He had a long list.

It was all automatic. Suddenly the children were gone and I was put together with some young people, about my age.

You had to roll up your sleeve and a Pole – his name was Bogdan – tattooed a number on your arm with a sort of pen.

Z 6084 was my number.[11]

At first I stayed in the main camp, in a school for masons. I knew some of the boys who worked there from Marzahn. We carted sand, learned how to mix cement and use a trowel, how to place the stones, where to put the pail so that the whole thing looked proper, some tricks of the trade. Since then I know how to lay bricks. It was something I mastered.[12]

But then they decided differently. I do not know how it came about. In any case, after a month, but it can also have been after only a few days, they said:

'Everybody line up! You, you, you, you, you.'

And then I, with some of the others, was moved over to Birkenau, to the gypsy camp Birkenau, as they called it.[13]

We marched in groups, always in single file, ran, got in line. Then it was immediately:

'Close up here! Close up there! You over there! You over there!'

You were pushed on and assigned to a block. At first I was sent to block three. A block, that was a barracks, all converted horse stables.[14] But you didn't say barracks, you said block.

The twenty-three or twenty-six blocks stood in two rows. A block was about ten metres long, maybe a bit longer, and four to five metres wide. The whole so-called gypsy camp was maybe one hundred metres wide and one hundred and fifty metres long.

Inside the blocks there were boxes out of boards, you can say wooden beds, always three, one on top of the other. A family or several people lived in each box. The beds, those were paper sacks that had been stuffed with wood-wool. The long-haired blankets with which we covered ourselves had been brought by our Jewish fellow-sufferers. In the middle there was a large stove, which was only laid after I had arrived. It was fed from two sides. But in winter it never got warm in the wooden barracks.

I had to report to the block senior. And later, during free time – before that nobody was allowed to leave the barracks, it was confinement to block – I asked around about which of our people were also there. I was unable to find out anything at first, but then, a few days later, I learned that my granny was there, that my sister Therese was there, that my cousins, my aunts and uncles, and also my brothers and sisters from my mother's second marriage were there.[15]

All of my uncles had been in the service. In the cavalry, the navy, the infantry. One cousin was in the air force.

One of them had fought with the mountain troops in Finland. While on furlough he had wanted to visit my grandmother in Marzahn.[16]

At the police station he had been told:

'Your mother is in the concert camp. They have been given a plot of land and they can build houses there and keep animals.'

Then my uncle had said:

'I do not want to fight for a country like this.'

They had taken his side-arm away and a fortnight later he was in Auschwitz.

In block three the senior was a Reichs German. Erich. I was with him for quite a while, he was all right.

During this time I searched for my granny and I found her.

'Oh, my boy!'

I strove to move to her block and achieved this most rapidly, with luck and some help.

My uncle Florian, the former hod-carrier, was block clerk there. He wrote down who was in the block, what there was in the way of food and so forth.

I then worked under the block senior Hans Koch, a man from Cologne, whom by the way I met again here in Berlin after the war, in the S-Bahn at the Sonnenallee station.

'You are Hans Koch!'

'No, no, no no. My name is Hans Walter Kaiser!'

But I had recognized him. He ran away, ran through the barrier and gone he was.

He had beaten me in the KZ. I was glad to be free. I would not have harmed him in any way.

An acquaintance from Marzahn, Günter, from Hamburg – he has also passed away in the meantime – and I had worked for him. We cleaned everything up and always got the place shipshape again. The SS had some sort of a room in his block and in the evening always brought in women, and the senior played along. They messed everything up and got drunk, and we always had to clean up the dirt and the crap. Naturally there were also unpleasant things, real filth, to get rid of. However, my laws forbade that. And I said:

'I will not do that. No, I will not do that!'

Then he took a stick and beat me and threw me out and reported me for refusing to work.

I did not know that such a statement would have such serious consequences for me. I was still new in Auschwitz and didn't even know that a block senior who sets the joint jumping had so much power. But I was soon to find out.

The block seniors were mainly Reich Germans and almost always professional criminals from the prisons and penitentiaries. They were the trusties of the SS, so to speak.

At the top was the camp senior, then his deputy, included were the clerks in the office. Then came the block senior, then the block clerk, then the room senior and the guard at the gate. These were all prisoners.

Naturally they were all under the SS, the camp commander and his deputy. The block senior reported to the block leader who was an SS man.

If somebody in the block messed things up the block seniors were also called to account. For example they had to crawl in pairs while a block leader or another SS man stood with a foot on each of their backs, and if they didn't go fast enough, then they got it with the whip. Then they had to get up and run.

'Get up! Move it!'

'Down!'

Do knee-bends, hop. Of course they became angry and hit out when they got back to their block.

They said:

'If this block ever attracts attention again I will beat the hell out of the whole block!'

The people trembled. Sometimes a block senior was only in a bad mood. Then it was enough if you just happened to be passing near.

'Hey, you too! Come here!'

On the other hand I have to say that the camp seniors and also the block seniors were far better off than on the outside. They could have everything they wanted, champagne or wine or women.

Everything was organized to a T. At work there was first the senior kapo, then the kapo, then the junior kapo, then the foremen, all of them prisoners who made sure that the people worked.

Each one had a specific responsibility, but each one also had a position that he could more or less exploit and fill in a different way. He could beat the people, but he could also treat then well. That was left up to the individual.

Some were moody. They treated the people just the way they themselves happened to feel. For example, if things didn't go the way they wanted during roll-call, then the whole block had to turn out. They let us stand for hours, men, women, and even the children. These roll-calls were always very hard on us.

I had not yet fully understood this camp, these camp regulations, what power a block senior had. He was unbelievably powerful, sort of the lord over life and death.

I was punished because of alleged refusal to work, I believe I was given a jacket and a red spot on the back and had to march out of the gypsy camp to the camp of the Jews.[17]

The camp of the Jews was a punishment camp, a camp with only men. There everything had to be done on the double. You were not allowed to stand still for even a minute.

'Move! Move! Move!'

If you were seen standing you immediately received a beating. You had to be on the move all the time.

'On the double! Move it, move it!'

Now I was young. But old men who were no longer able, they did not live long.

Things were also strict in the gypsy camp, but in the punishment camp everything was much worse.

There when you heard:

'Turn out!' everybody ran for their lives.

If somebody was a little late, even in the morning he got his thrashing. Some were constantly being beaten because they attracted attention for their poor work. Maybe they were only sick, but nobody cared about that.

'Lazy dog. We'll teach you.'

We carried sand and stones from here to there and from there to here, only with a shovel because there was no pannier, always in a triangle. For the most part this was completely senseless work. But we also unloaded wagons, cement and stones. Each of us had a bag of cement loaded on his back and if you did not move off quickly enough you got another one loaded on top. That was then a hundred kilos. My legs almost broke off.

We also converted former horse stables into barracks. The floor was dug out. We carried in sand in plasterers' panniers. These were already heavy enough. Over the sand we put gravel, then boards, then clay. We also built the boxes.

The camp of the Jews was directly next to the gypsy camp. One day I went to the electric fence and saw my granny on the other side. She called:

'Come to the fence in the evening!'

I went and she threw across a wrapped loaf of bread for me. I thought the bread came from my uncle Florian, the block clerk. But it was her bread. This I only learned when I was back with her again. I had a quarrel with him about it:

'You can easily get hold of some bread. Yet you let Mammy throw her own bread across!'

Once my uncle was assigned by the block senior to put together a huge pack of bread and throw it across the fence for somebody else. That person did not appear. I was there instead. My uncle therefore threw it to me. That was a real feast.

When my grandmother again threw something across the fence for me, one of the block leaders saw me. She just held her eyes shut and ran away. He beat me, but not on the backside or the shoulders, but always in between. With every blow I fell down.

'Get up!'

On and on. He beat the hell out of me. You were not allowed to talk across the fence. But I had simply thought: bread is life.

I fell ill. I became sick and fell down. Some Sinti who knew me took me to the infirmary with the medic. Some said it was typhoid, some spotted fever, others malaria. What it actually was I can no longer say for certain today.

The block senior there was called Rosin, Ernst, I remember that clearly. Also a nice man.

You can be surrounded by the worst kind of devils, but there are always one or two people among them who are good.

The infirmary barracks in the Jews' camp were not made out of wood. They were small, low stone huts. But with the same wooden boxes.

My senses left me, I could hardly breathe and broke out in sweat. Most of the time I just dozed away. My mouth was all cracked from the fever. Sometimes someone came by and gave me a spoonful of a white paste.

'Good, go back to sleep.'

Either you got well or you didn't. Nobody gave a damn either way. Next to me in the box there was a Dutchman or a Belgian who received packages. The third man was already gone, he was already dead. There were two of us. Now my neighbour kept repeating:

'Water, water, water.'

I knew that he had a package, but he didn't give me anything. I said:

'I'll get water for you, but then you have to give me something.'

We were only allowed to drink tea. Drinking water was forbidden. Whoever got water and drank and was caught at it was beaten to death, because the water was infected with typhoid. They wanted to prevent the typhoid from spreading.

I had a red cup that could be tied on. And with this cup under my prison coat I then slowly moved out of the box to the bathroom. The water was always shut off, but I knew how to get some. You had to open the tap and suck at it and as soon as you felt the water, to block the pipe with your tongue. Then I held the cup underneath. Some water always dripped out. What I had sucked out and held in my mouth I also spat into the cup. When it was half full I slowly moved back towards my box again, climbed up, put the cup down and shook my neighbour:

'Hey you, I have brought you water!'

And he was dead. He was really dead! Oh, I thought, my God! But the thought came to me immediately: now you can just take his package.

But I had to watch out that the room senior who occasionally looked in did not notice anything. I carefully pulled the package from under the corpse and slowely but surely took out everything I needed until the food inside was almost all gone. The rest I put under my pillow. But I left the package as it was. Only then did I call the room senior. At the time the room senior was a Pole.

'Stubowi! Stubowi! There is a dead one here!'

'Throw out!' he said.

Well sure, 'throw out'! That wasn't possible, I could not lift the dead man! So I did that with my feet, always pushing him a bit further towards the front until he was right up on the edge, and then I gave him a shove. He fell out on the floor. They took him by the legs and dragged him away – bam bam bam bam, the head always bumped on the ground like that.

The package again gave me the necessary strength and uplift. After another week I felt better. I was able to leave the infirmary and worked outside the camp.

In the morning we were awakened by an iron slab that hung outside in front of the block. It sounded like a triangle.

We marched out and did levelling. Here there was no more wire, there were only guards. We cleared out old stuff, cardboard and such, and burned all kinds of things.

During this work a boy went too near to the line of guards and was shot. Later we carried him back in on a door. They said he had tried to escape, but all he wanted was to pick some sorrel, those long thin leaves.

I ate them too. If you had several leaves you rolled them together and pushed them into your cheek just to have some kind af taste.

The boy had dared to go quite a way close to the line of guards and then this vagabond shot him.

See, that was how things went.

After a while I came to a decision. I reported in.

'Z 6084 requests permission to go to the office!'

And who did I find there? Camp commander Schwarzhuber.[18] A wiry thin man.

'Z 6084 present and reporting! Permission to make a request!'

I told him that I came from Berlin and that my granny was over in the gypsy camp and that I would like to go there.

'Goiman?' he said. 'You speak Goiman so good!'

'Yes, I am from Berlin.'

But always in fear. He looked at me and asked me some more questions. And I answered everything.

'Well', he said, 'if that is not true we are going to have a little chat.'

'Jawoll!'

To your prison dress you had a cap on and always when an SS man went by, no matter who that was, you had to immediately rip the cap from your head, arms at your side and start marching and your eyes directed at him and then say your number and report if there was anything to report. If there was nothing you had to march past him like that. And he looked at your number. If he noted it down, then you were in for it.

That was the way I stood before Schwarzhuber. And he said that if what I had told him was true I would be sent over.

Now I didn't really pin any great hopes on that. And suddenly, one morning, my number was called up:

'Z 6084 to the office!'

I thought:

'Well, now you have forfeited your life.'

'Is approved, can go over.'

Nothing more. Schwarzhuber himself wasn't even present.

'Approved, can go over.'

There were several of us.

'Attention! In step march!

Just like soldiers. Oh was I happy! The relief! And so I came back to my granny. I thought to myself:

'There you will get an extra helping of food, there you can get hold of stuff.'

VI

I then became the door guard in my grandmother's block. Before the block senior Wally took me on, he hit me five times with a baton and said:

'You will get another taste of this if you let somebody out of here without my permission. When there is confinement to block then nobody is allowed out.'

Whoever did not work had to spend the whole day in his block. This included the older people who did not work because of their children. They were given free time. During free time you could take a walk on the camp street for a while, or quickly slip away somewhere to visit somebody or other.

You were also allowed to use the toilet during this time, a barrack in the centre of which there were rows of concrete holes. You had to ... opposite, next to each other ... Most were sick. That was so terrible. Women pulled a cloth over their face, but it was terrible. Here one of the greatest taboos was broken. It was not a normal way of relieving yourself but a torture and insult to our people.

They cut off all our hair, under the arms too and also the pubic hair. The same shears were also used to shave the head, the beard.

Those are things that even today, when you talk about them, they still hurt very much.

Later on, when I worked in the sauna and saw my grand-mother as she held the little one in front of herself like that, then I turned away. I knew how embarrassing it was for her, in front of her grandson. Women with their grown-up sons and men, naked in front of their daughters – there can be no greater torment.

A gong signalled the end of free time and everybody had to be back in the block. Whoever was not in, who came late or was caught on the camp street by the block leaders was heavily punished.

'Where were you? What block?'

Some were shot on the spot, others were taken to their block, laid across the stove and beaten with sticks or whips.

As door guard things were quite all right until one day a woman came along with her child. She insisted on going to the toilet with him.

I said:

'I am not allowed to let anybody out.'

Her husband joined us and made a scene. I don't know, I'm a human being, if somebody talks nicely to me, even if I know what I might be in for. Finally I said:

'Well, OK. But please do that very carefully! Watch out that you are not caught. And if you are caught then don't say I let you out!'

And what happened? They were caught.

'Where did you get out from?'

Then they came for me, the SS man and the block senior. They gave me at least twenty or twenty-five blows with a stick for that.

I had to count along and just couldn't take any more. They hit me between pelvis and back. Afterwards I could neither lie down nor sit nor stand. You simply can't describe something like that.

I kept my job as door guard, but I never again let anybody out.

The upshot was that I then had trouble with this woman's husband.

They had also been beaten, by the block senior. I believe the child as well, but I don't want to say anything that is wrong.

'It is your fault, it was you who said that I had let you out!'

The man thereupon took a hooked knife and threatened me. My cousin Oscar went at him with a cudgel and beat him up. At that moment the block senior Wally showed up.

'What's going on. Oscar?'

Oscar told him. And then this man got such a beating from the block senior that from then on he left me alone.

Oscar was a sort of supervisor in our block. He was not very kind to the people. Very strict. When he walked over to the stove and somebody made a false move, this person immediately got a beating. If Oscar had survived Auschwitz he would have met certain people who would have knocked him off. I would not have wished that on him. After all, he was my cousin.

I survived Auschwitz and can go to anybody. I never hurt anyone. I was content if nobody hurt me.

Of course I also had a cudgel. When some people hung over the food barrel and stuck their heads inside so as to get out the leavings, it could happen that I brandished it.

'Will you stop that!

Then they ran away and I took my cup.

And then I had to get a move on because they came back. Today I laugh about it, but back then it was dead serious.

People who worked in the kitchen organized a few potatoes in a pot. When the block senior was away I took the lid off the stove – the stoves were long and continuous and had two stacks – pushed the pot inside and closed the lid again. If the block senior had caught me he would have strung me up. When the potatoes were done I got some. That was my sideline during my time as door guard. That helped me to get by.

Whoever was right at the bottom and had nobody to give him a little help, irrevocably went under. Whoever was being beaten was already marked. Whoever was emaciated, out of whose eyes death already stared, provoked so much aggression that he was beaten even more until one day he was dead. Somebody like that didn't stand a chance. The only one who had a chance was someone who did not go sick, who was able to work. As the sign said : 'Work makes free!' And then 'Extermination through work'. And that was really true. They let people work so long and hard, until all their strength was gone.

The food was very bad. In the morning we received tea from the room senior out of a kettle and a quarter of a loaf of bread. But they cheated us on this too. The bread was cut into quarters but a big slice was cut out of the middle, which was then distributed to the children.

There was hardly any real lunch, only with nettles and pieces of cabbage in it, real dish-water. You couldn't draw any strength from that.

I believe I lost the job as door guard later on because we were moved to another block.

In any case I then worked for a Pole. He was a big man, was called Jurek, and was totally drunk every day. How he managed that I have no idea. He always had cigarettes and drink and got food from the kitchen. So much to eat, meat! When he was out I took the lid off and...

Once he noticed that there was too little food. He beat the hell out of me and threw me out. But I could not resist. I accepted the beating, because at least I was full.

I fell ill again. I got scabies, from my face to my feet. I was no longer able to work. I could no longer close my fingers. Pimples, pus. Terrible. They treated me with 'mitigal', a white, milky fluid. You see, this was also a bad time, and yet it too passed.

Do you want to know what always makes me so pensive: why did I survive? I do not know the answer to that myself. The whole family, all of my brothers and sisters, everyone who was very dear to me, not one person was able to survive. Even though my brothers were much stronger and tougher than I. I was the smallest! I cannot understand that. They say: you have your freedom now, be happy. There was no way I could be all that joyful, because I missed my brothers and sisters, always, to this very day. When the holidays came and people celebrated, or the families sat together, that was when this inner thing, this nervous strain came. That was very hard.

At the block senior's, Hans Koch, I had met a woman, Sonja. She is still alive. Her son has actually come to see me once or twice. We played cards together.

With Koch she had been a clerk, block clerk. We got along well together. I never did her any harm, nor she me.

'What are you doing, Piepel?' she asked me.

That's what they all called me because I was still so small.

'I'm not doing anything. You know that Koch threw me out, beat me, I was sent to the punishment battalion, but thank God I am now back here again due to the camp commander. And now I have been thrown out again.'

'Oh, do you know what? I will ask Kapo Felix. Maybe he can use you.'

Kapo Felix was doing it with her sister, she did his clerical work for him.

She actually did ask – and – 'Jawoll!' – then I got the job of runner for the sauna.

This was a barracks on the site of the gypsy camp, with a disinfection facility, a bathing facility, and a sauna.[19] The sauna was not there to take off weight – we were all skinny enough – but to clean ourselves. There were showers, real ones, without gas, and there I really proved myself. I was again able to stabilize myself.

With Kapo Felix everything was well ordered. I got up in the morning, left my block, went to my job, and when that was over I returned to my block. I worked for this Kapo Felix until July 1944, up until my transfer to Buchenwald.

Unfortunately I do not know what became of him. He was a strong, hefty man, but I never saw him beat or insult anybody. I believe he was a political prisoner.[20] Anyway, a Reichs German.

I delivered reports, but also did shopping for him – lunch, coffee or tea. This gave me a small chance to support my siblings, the three brothers and two sisters from my mother's second marriage.

When I went to fetch lunch I always passed by the block of my brothers and sisters. You never had time for others. My person was always only at work and after work it was not possible to go here or there.

Finally I thought to myself:

'Oh, why don't you just try it!'

With the tin in which I fetched the food for the kapo I went into the block to my brothers and sisters, poured some food into their bowls and then went back to the kitchen a second time.

'The kapo would like seconds.'

They just gave me a second helping without any questions. And since this had worked once, I did it again and again at intervals.

All this was just a drop in a bucket. My brothers and sisters were under sentence of death, there was nothing to be done about it. Every time I came in, when they saw me, the yammer! They would all have liked to get out with me. But that was not possible. You could not help anybody directly, only indirectly.

When I talk about my siblings I mean my oldest sister, a daughter of my father from his first marriage, my sister Therese, who grew up together with me at my granny, and the five children my mother had with her second husband, of whom the eldest, Harry, was about ten years old.

The children were also tattooed, on the thigh.

My eldest sister Drosla, in other words my half-sister who had stayed with my father when I came to Berlin, I really only saw consciously for the first time in Birkenau. I believe her name was Dembrowski. She had married and had several children.[21]

We found out that we were siblings quite by accident, in a conversation with other people. I mentioned the names of my parents and she came to me and embraced me.

'Spatzo, you are my brother!'

She stayed in Auschwitz, with her husband and all her children. Not one of them made it.

Of course I was glad to have met her, but basically I could not help her either. We were in deep misery and everybody had his duty which he had to fulfil without fail. But we did see each other from time to time and talked about my father.

I do not know how it was possible that I survived Auschwitz. To this very day I don't see why. I was just lucky. Some protecting hand had probably been held over me.

The policy of the camp leadership was to tear the families apart, to divide them. In the end, all that was left was to think about yourself, no longer to think of others. That is how it came about that the father would eat the bread of his child.

In a KZ which is not a family camp, everybody makes sure that he keeps what he gets, because he knows it is his chance for survival. A piece of bread is worth more in an KZ than a thousand-mark note. You can't eat that. A piece of bread or a potato. You are dependent on every little bit they offer you and you also have to have courage. If you see that you have a chance to get something, then you have to muster all your courage to do it. I was beaten several times. I had to take this into account when I went to the kitchen to get something or other, for example potato peels or later on in Ellrich food the army threw away. I grabbed it, put it in my cap and ran. If they caught me, my number was written down. Either I was beaten immediately, or I was called up later, by number. But I did not care, the main thing was that I had something to eat.

My sister Therese also stayed in Auschwitz. But she was not gassed. She had that valvular defect in her heart and she died of that. She was burned, but not gassed.

Once I went to the crematoria with kapo Felix and had a look at all that.

We left the gypsy camp, under SS guard of course, went to the crematorium and there got those round tins, with that Cyclon B. Two or three times. I accompanied kapo Felix, not only to look but to help carry.

'Come with me,' he had said.

I did not see the gas showers, but the ovens and the wagons on which the dead were driven to the ovens.

We took the tins and went back to our camp.

We had a serrated chisel, a round piece of iron with teeth. I set this against the centre of the tin and hit it with a hammer. Then the tin part was broken out and removed and then you could take these quadrilateral crystals out that looked turquoise, or blue.

A few crystals were enough to delouse enormous piles of blankets and clothing.

We all went through the delousing. By block.[22] Men and women. But I do not want to say anything here that is wrong. I believe the men came first to the delousing and then the women. But I no longer recall this exactly. I believe that on kapo Felix's initiative men and women were separated later on.

In any case you first waded through a pool with a solution against bacteria or fungi. When the people were in there, kapo

Felix turned the water on. Then they had a shower. And in the meantime their clothes which they had taken off before were deloused. These things were hung in a wagon and put separately through a steambath and were pushed out again on the other side. There the people took them again and got dressed.

That is how it went, block by block, and when the last block was through you started again at the beginning.

I never saw anything like that later. So many lice, so much stuff, animals! It was not as if you could scrape them together by hand! You had to use a shovel. Yes, that was how many lice there were, and at each delousing! If you shook out the blankets they fell out like sand. That is how many there were.

It just crawled, it just crawled with them.

And to keep this under control, that is what the sauna was for.

Among others the camp leaders, the labour assignment leaders, the block leaders also came, but that was SS. Yes, they came too. They took showers and put down their shoes or boots. I had to clean these and then they were put back in their place. Everything fine. You see I had a wonderful job.

The Canada Command also came to us. They called that the Canada Command.[23]

These were the people whose job it was to kill the people with the gas and then to burn them in the ovens. They were replaced every six weeks. Either because they were then no longer able, or because nothing was to get out outside.

The Jews who arrived were not even first taken into the camp. They arrived in Birkenau behind our fence, on the tracks. There the families were sorted into children and mothers, young people, older people. Cases and everything else they had to leave there. They were told they would go to the showers – it's true, by far the most of them were sent into the gas showers and were then burned. They did not even realize what was happening to them. They were told they would go into a shower and in fact this stuff, this Cyclon B, was dumped in from above, and then the water was turned on. It only turned into a gas in connection with water. And that is the way all of these people were killed.

You knew what was going on there, everybody knew it. Once a commission came to our camp and asked the children what those ovens and chimneys were back over there. The crematoria were only a few hundred metres away. And the children said:

'That is where the bread is baked.'

They were afraid they would be killed if they told the truth.[24]

The newcomers who were able to work were divided up among the various camps, where others had died or where more labour was required.

The Canada Command broke out the people's teeth, they took off their rings and other things. I do not know what other kinds of things they did to the people.

This command always worked very closely with the SS people. The Jews brought along lots of gold and jewels and money and this and that, the best soaps, perfume, lipsticks and so forth. And when the Canada Command came to us in the sauna to delouse themselves and take a shower and have their clothes disinfected, then I had to hang these in the wagons. Of course I looked into the pockets, at all the things that were in them. The people of the command came out of the sauna on the other side, they did not come back to us in the camp. If I had taken everything out there would still not have been anything they could have done about it. But I only took little things which I could use, which I thought, you can trade them, biscuits or such. And when you bit into such a biscuit you sometimes found a small ring or a little piece of a chain. The Jews had baked all that into the biscuits.

The people of the Canada Command were given the best food, lived like kings, and also slept very well. However, when the six weeks were over, then they went along into the ovens too. I do not know if they knew that, but in any case our kapo Felix told us that. And he was a Reichs German.

The Reichs Germans were condemned prisoners too, but they were not treated as renegades like us. We were no longer allowed to be Germans. They had a lot of clout. They also did black-market traffic with the SS. Especially the Canada Command. The things that arrived there, so much gold and money and things! The most beautiful fur coats that were taken from the Jewish women were later worn by SS wives.

Camp commanders, work force leaders, they all came to us. One of the work force leaders who came to us in the sauna limped. A big man. He walked with a crutch. The children always ran to him and touched him.

Dr Mengele also came to us, he took showers in the sauna too. I cleaned the dust from his boots and set them down for him.

When it became known that Dr Mengele was coming, the children all ran to him. He took them by the hand and went behind the sauna with them, because the infirmary building was directly in front of the sauna.

His driver – sometimes Dr Mengele also drove himself – came in an open cross-country car. At the back in the storage space all sorts of glasses were lying about. Big ones, small ones, tall ones. You could see that they were filled with different kinds of things. What these were I cannot say.

In front of the infirmary Dr Mengele always put on his white gown. Then he went in.

Once I also visited the infirmary. On some people they had cut into their flesh above or below the knee, and a bit further on cut it again and then pulled a piece of gauze through with a long pair of scissors. What that was for? I do not know. The people all got swollen faces or swollen feet. Whoever was put in there did not come out again That I know. My uncle lay in there. His wife too. Neither of them came out again. Another uncle too. They were all destroyed.

I cannot say that Dr Mengele gave somebody a lethal injection. I was not there. You heard about that, but I do not know if it was true. He was a good-looking, imposing man and very friendly, always laughing, never angry. If you looked at him he always had a friendly look. He was always laughing.

Afterwards they called him the death angel of Auschwitz, because when he appeared, then death was programmed. He looked at the people and marked them, and then they were taken away, either because of contagious disease or I do not know for what other reasons. He was always particularly interested in twins. Thank God I was not included.

He came to us in the sauna, took a shower and freshened up. I polished his boots and set them down. He drew them on and chatted with the kapo. I did not speak with him. I had to do everything on orders like a soldier.

76

'Z 6084! Everything in order!'

'Yesyesyes.'

That was all he said. Then he left. Once he left some cigarettes behind, deliberately. He was not permitted to give anybody anything, that we knew. But I'm sure he gave the kapo something, and he him too. Both of them, you know, were great, you could almost say, friends. And that is the way it was with the top people too. When the two of them talked I was not allowed to be present. This always took place behind a door, in the office.[25] I couldn't hear anything. On the other hand it did not interest me at all. There was nothing I could have changed anyway.

Mengele was the kind of person to whom all the others had to come. I would never have believed that he in any way wanted anything evil. Later, after 1945, I heard more about him.

I knew about the experiments. That he removed organs from people there, that I knew. All the prisoners knew that:

'Here he comes again. Now he is going to take what he needs again.'

But 'removing organs' was never spoken about. They said: he is taking things out of the corpses again to do experiments. That is what we called it. 'Removing organs', that is only the way it is expressed today.

I believe that if doctors then had been as advanced as they are today with the removal of organs then, none of us would have been worked to death. Quite the opposite. They would have said: we don't want you, but you will all be interned. We would all have led wonderful lives, with the best food and drink, with sports, with entertainment and so forth. They would have said: for your inner life, for your soul, we will care as well, and we can always fall back on you whenever we want. So that then, when the organs were needed, they could have said: well, it's his turn tomorrow. Then they would really have had perfectly fresh goods, and that would never have run out, masses of people you lavish care and attention on, who are constantly under medical supervision, every blood group, all of them people where you know exactly whose heart fits in whom and so forth. That would have become one of the best meat banks.

That would at least have been better. They would not have gassed and burned millions.

I do not know whether today if I were to walk by a pile of corpses I would be so totally without feelings, but at Birkenau I had got used to it. The corpses were part of our daily routine. They were just there, and we had to see them. They were impossible to overlook. And it did not make me feel bad so that I might have said: Oh, those poor people. There lay men, women and children.

I can remember a man, I believe he was a Czech Roma, who together with somebody else picked the corpses up by an arm and a leg and they were tossed up on the lorry like wood. The corpses of children they picked up by an arm or a leg and twirled them through the air just as if you were throwing something away. The bodies whirled about and flew onto the lorry.

The corpse pile was directly next to the sauna behind the infirmary. The dead were dragged there. Piled up. Stored. Stacked. Dumped. Always up, always up. All naked. Every evening the pile was over two metres high. And every evening a lorry with trailer came to collect this pile and drive it to the crematorium.

You don't feel anything any more. The people become, how should I say, unfeeling. They feel nothing any more. If somebody had come and stood them up against the wall they would not have said:

'No, help!'

They would not have cried or screamed either, no, nothing. In our condition we would have let anything be done to us, like lambs that are taken to the slaughter. Just like that. That is what we had come to.

In a situation like that people lose their feeling for human beings. All they do is kick, beat up, and take away to enrich themselves, to survive. And if you then take a real look at man at the very end and study him, which I did, then you see: those are no longer human beings, they are like animals, they have an expression on their faces that you can no longer define.

You can no longer tell about anyone whether he intends good or bad. Everybody is already so far gone with his nerves and thoughts, can't see anybody else any longer. If he has the ability to knock somebody dead, then he knocks him dead. He has no inner feeling any more. You saw that with the kapos and with the SS too. It made no difference whether it was a woman or a child or a man, they hit them on the head until the blood spurted and even then they sometimes kept on hitting. Here you can no longer speak about human beings.

The SS raped our women. Not directly inside the block, but mostly behind the block or some place else, and afterwards they shot them. One of my relatives they also shot in the head. In here and out of the head again there. She is still alive, but there are moments when she is unapproachable. And one dare not remind her of those times.

Behind the sauna there was a ditch with water, then the fence and behind the fence were the guards, in front of the tracks. To this ditch some children went. It was warm and the children were supposed to fetch water to clean the block. And then one of the guards shot at them and hit them too. One in the arm, a little boy in the stomach. I saw that myself, saw how the boy clutched at his guts.

That immediately led to them ordering a confinement to block.

There were people who broke out. Among others these were electricians who knew all about the electric fence, when it was shut off. The camp fence was under high tension.

I remember a Sinto who was caught. First his parents, the father, the mother, and his brothers and sisters who were all in the same block were given a good and proper beating. He was brought back. They dressed him in a completely new, completely clean prisoner's outfit and then he was pulled across the trestle.

The trestle, this was slats with a bulge, similar to the contraption with which farmers used to sort potatoes, except that there was a box underneath into which you had to put your feet at a twist so that you could not pull them back out again. You had to lie across it in the hollow, and on the left and right somebody pulled tight on your hands. And from behind two men then began beating, with thick leather whips. In the beginning it was the SS, but later on the SS apparently no longer fancied it. Then the kapos or block seniors had to do it. And then you could see how the blood ran down the back of the trousers of the one being beaten.

They tortured the Sinto who had attempted to escape to death. They laid him on a door and first showed him on the parade ground and then carried him from block to block so that we could see: this will happen to anybody who tries to break out here. As a deterring example. And I believe that after that nobody else tried to do a bunk. Already for the sake of the family. Would have been nonsense anyway. They would have caught you again everywhere. You did not know where you could have turned to.

So we had all become completely apathetic. And despite this, on one occasion we resisted.

They intended to burn us, us Sinti. All of us.

They had already taken out the Russian Sinti in Block 23, they had burned them.[26] They had told us that they had had smallpox and would infect us. Towards evening a few lorries drove in. The SS jumped down with dogs, carbines and machine-guns and beat the people up into the lorries. We could hear the screams and the barking and the shots. We also looked out through the skylights. There were no real windows in the barracks.

The cars drove away and then we saw how the flames leapt up out of the chimneys of the crematorium, and it smelled of burnt human flesh. Whether these people were gassed or shot I can't say. In Auschwitz you no longer noticed whether a machine-gun hammered away, whether shots rang out.

I had had a girl friend in that block, a Roma, the daughter of the block senior. His name was Didi, her name was Sofie, and I had gone to see her that day.

When the block seniors learned that we Sinti and Roma were all going to be burned they said – and there you have to give him credit, Hans Koch, and all the other block seniors,

Wally, that was a short, blond, husky one, a real dog, but still – he also lived with one of our Sinti women – then the block seniors said:

'Now pay attention. The camp commander intends to come in here and round up the Sinti here.'

I was to take up position on one side of the camp street opposite the sauna, and my cousin Oscar – the one I went to school with – on the other side.

The block seniors said to us:

'When we give you the signal with the torches you dash off and knock on every block. They will know what to do.'

If the SS had seen us they would have shot us. But they did not see us. When we then saw the blinking signal we dashed off and when we knocked, the block senior of every block knew: Aha, here they come.

We slipped back into our barracks again. And then it did not take long, here came camp commander Schwarzhuber and his men marching into the camp with leashed dogs and machine-guns. He marched past several blocks with his men.

'Block senior reports block 7 occupied by 350 prisoners! Nothing to report!'

He came inside to us briefly. Allegedly all he wanted to do was to check file cards. Samples.

We knew what was really going on. We were all armed, shovel, spade, hammer, pick, hoe, pitchfork, with our work tools and whatever people had found. The people said to themselves: very well, if they want to round us up here, then we will sell our lives as dearly as possible. We will not put ourselves in their hands. Maybe we will get to the machine-guns, then we will naturally have a better chance.

In the main that was the block seniors, the room seniors, all those who were still quite strong.

Schwarzhuber noticed that the lights had gone on in all the barracks, and also over in the Poles' camp and the Jews' camp, and that all of Birkenau was lit up. Everybody was wide awake.

Many of the block seniors and kapos were having affairs with our women. There were children born there too. Therefore they did not want the extermination. They were ready to fight along with us. So this was dangerous for the SS.

And so Schwarzhuber checked on a few blocks and then marched off with his troops just as he had marched in, without further ado, because he said to himself: if we do that there is going to be chaos, they will not give up, they will resist. Maybe they would have shot fifty or a hundred of us, but then we would have gone for Schwarzhuber. He would not have got out in one piece.

The people, almost all of whom had by now lived in Birkenau for two years or more knew what the game was. It was not like with the Jews who arrived from other countries and put their suitcases down.

The action was cancelled and we remained in Auschwitz.[27]

Until August 1944. Then there was a move. They said: all the people who are still able to work will be shipped out, among others also Otto Rosenberg – also to be shipped out. Sort of according to the motto:

'Show me your muscles, and if you're fit then you can work.'

At first I did not want to go.

'Mammy I will stay with you.'

There were already so many grandchildren there whose parents were already gone and who all clung to granny.

'Come along,' I said.

'No, I cannot leave the children on their own here. It is impossible for me to leave the children. Their fear – no, I will stay here my boy and you go.'

And then she herself said:

'Here, room senior, here is another one, my boy wants to go along too.'

And all the time I didn't want to go. And she immediately:

'Go, go, out!'

And then I went along. My cousin Oscar and his younger brother Bodo came along. And as we found out later, their father too, my mother's brother Florian, as well as my uncle Julius.

First we went to the main camp at Auschwitz and had to wait. And then the shipment left for Buchenwald.[28]

VII

In Buchenwald we were sent before a camp doctor. He sat behind a table. We had to get in line and take everything off. He looked at us and with a gesture assigned us to a side.

Oscar was sent to one side with me. Bodo was sent to the other.

Then they said the side Bodo was on was to be sent back to Auschwitz.

He was probably too weak. But at the most he was only one year younger than we were. Bodo began to cry. He had always been together with his brother.

Then Oscar went across to his brother and exchanged his number with another boy who wanted to stay in Buchenwald.

The number from Auschwitz was no longer valid in Buchenwald. We had already been given new numbers. I had number 74669. However, the number was not tattooed in but was only on the clothes. We had had to sew them on our trousers and on our jackets top left.

Oscar exchanged this number and with this went back to Auschwitz with his brother Bodo to his death. I believe he knew that. The younger people who went back to Auschwitz were all sent to their destruction there.[29]

I do not know whether I too would not have acted like Oscar if my brother would have gone back and I would have had the chance of going with him. But I was always alone. My mother was in the KZ at Ravensbrück. And my father and my brother Waldemar were at Bialystok in a KZ, and my brother Max in the KZ Neuengamme. I was only together with granny, and that only for part of the time. And I believe that it was all for the best that I was alone. I did not have to make allowances for anybody. What I wanted to do, that I decided for myself and did it too. That was one reason why I survived.

That is the way the friends from my childhood went away. But it was not so that you could have said:

'Take care!'

Or with a leave-taking or such. There was none of that at all.

'Line up! That way! That way!'

And like this.

'Well, so long.'

Finished.

What was going to happen to those concerned was easy to imagine, but you really didn't think about it. Anybody who had spent two years in Auschwitz like I had, had developed a certain apathy. We let everything happen to us without resisting. They gave us an injection up here where the heart is. Nobody reared up. Nobody said:

'No, we won't allow you to do that.'

We did not know what it was. And we did not give any thought to it either. We were already so apathetic that we did not care.

Maybe it was a vaccination. It must have been a vaccination or I would not be sitting here.

We then learned from the block seniors who came later that the rest of us who had stayed in Auschwitz, among others my grandmother, but also all the other cousins and grandchildren, that the whole gypsy camp at Birkenau had been liquidated. Everything finished. They killed them all.

How long we stayed in Buchenwald I do not know exactly. Was it one week, was it three weeks, a fortnight? I don't know.

There was a bear-pen there, with a bear in it. The man who tended it was named Itzig.

The kapos and block seniors in Buchenwald settled accounts with the kapos and block seniors from Auschwitz who had beaten relatives or friends of the Buchenwalders. They knew everything that had taken place in Auschwitz. They interrogated the foremen from Auschwitz and gave them beatings. One they almost beat to death. Whether he had killed a pregnant women or kicked her in the stomach, that I don't recall. He was already down on the ground and one of them wanted to drop a huge rock on his head. At the last moment he was able to evade it. He jumped up and then he was beaten again and again, ran for his life, and disappeared between the rows. He was lucky.

I was put to work. We had to go down, very far down into a deep quarry. There each of us took a stone on his shoulder and with this we had to climb the long, long way back up. We threw the stone down and climbed back down again without any delay. It was a circulation, a chain. The work was hard because the stones were jagged and often really huge.

The camp leader did not know what else to do with the people except to keep them occupied.

And then suddenly they said: on again.

Again they put a shipment together, again I was selected, and this shipment was sent to Dora.

Dora was in the Harz. There they were building the shafts in which the V2, the miracle weapon, was manufactured.[30]

We were employed as shaft clearers. Many worked inside in the shaft, with pneumatic drills.

I first worked outside the shaft. We drove a trench into the stone. Holes were drilled into the rock, then cartridges were put in, then they blasted, and then the debris was cleared out.

The kapo was from Berlin. His name was Hundekopp. He had a totally bent nose. He had probably been a boxer or a barman. A real giant.

At Dora I met a cousin who, while also coming from Auschwitz, had never come to my attention there.

Together with him and my two uncles I was then soon sent to Ellrich.[31]

VIII

Assembly call.

'Everybody line up!'

We lined up, sounded off by number and were then distributed among the stone barracks. Three or four men were given one blanket together with paper sacks which were filled with wood-wool, full of fleas and crap. We slept, and next morning there was half a loaf of bread. But these were small loaves, coarse wholemeal bread. And jam. For lunch there was boiled potatoes and herring. But there was no water. And in the evening again half a loaf and sometimes a slice of sausage or cheese. But a quarter of a loaf was not a quarter of a loaf. As in Auschwitz the bread was divided in the middle and lengthwise, and when doing this the dogs always cut a big slice out of the middle. So a quarter of a loaf was only an eighth of a loaf, and of course that was not enough.

We had to line up by block. Then the work teams were put together. Some worked inside the shaft, others outside.

I was assigned to the 'gawabau', the gas-water-instalment on level two. We worked outside the shaft and shovelled the debris into the cars. Then we laid the pipes for the water and the drainage. Over mountains and through valleys. I also worked on the rock-face, with the pneumatic drill. We had to go eighty centimetres deep into the ground and the rock as I recall. Of course that was very hard work. I was very lucky that I did not smoke.

At three o'clock, four o'clock, just as they felt like it, we had to line up. Every morning we marched out of the KZ. A Sinti band played.

'Lift your legs!'

Just like soldiers.

'Detachment halt! In step, march! On the double, march!'

Or marking time.

We marched a short way, to the station, a flat building. There we got onto cattle cars, always in assigned groups.

'Into the wagons!'

Then you had to hurry. Woe to anybody who was not inside quick enough! Those in the rear always got it. Blows. The Russians joined us in the wagon. We rode to the Woffleben station.[32]

It was different getting off.

'Out!'

Then things quieted down a bit. The train drove off. We crossed the tracks and marched to a big circular area. There we had to line up again and when we were all present we were allowed to march off in groups to our place of work.

I worked under kapo Keutmann. We called him Katschka, that is Polish, it means 'duck', because he had such bowed legs and always waddled back and forth like that. The Russians or the Poles had dubbed him so.

At noon we all met again at the assembly place. But sometimes not. Then we got our lunch at our place of work. Nettles with cabbage, potatoes, turnips, carrots, such dish-water. One ladleful. There were bowls, but they were always collected again, to wash in. The Russians called these bowls *miski*. You always had to exert yourself to get a hold of one of these *miski*. You had to stand in line with it and you held it out. Then the one who was passing out the food dipped the ladle in and when he lifted it out half spilled out. You then got what was left. If you said something you got the ladle on your head. So you said nothing.

After lunch we marched back to our place of work. At the assembly area there was an iron bar, a piece of railway track, I believe, that hung from a branch.

'Dingdingdingding!'

Whoever was not at his place of work immediately was searched for and beaten. Everybody was punctual, nobody dared to go too far off.

After work we all assembled at the area again. Lining up in rows of two or three.

'Dress lines! Eyes to the front! In step, march!'

Then came the checks. The command stopped. Jabs.

'You out, you out, you out!'

These were then searched. If something was found there were beatings.

When it grew colder we took empty cement sacks and cut holes in the sides and the top. Then we put them on and over them our shirt.

When we marched the guards always hit us on the back with a stick. Slap, slap. That way they heard whether there was a cement bag underneath.

'Out! Out!'

'Strip!'

If you had a bag on you were beaten. Then your number was noted, there was no way out. They said it was because of the cement scabies. But I don't know. I cleaned my bag, really shook it out and turned it inside out. No wind got through, the bag kept you warm.

Our feet were also checked. There were no stockings. But sometimes somebody tore a blanket and then the others joined in. You then wrapped it around your feet as a foot-cloth. Thank God I was never caught.

At the time I had a pilot's cap out of leather which I had traded for at one time or another, with ear-flaps. That was actually my good luck.

In Ellrich we had to fall in again, and then off to the bathroom. Then tea, move on, bread, off.

Then there was still a little time, when it was warm, to take a walk in the camp grounds. Towards evening there was another bell, then everybody had to be in their boxes.

Next morning the whole thing began all over again. A bell. 'Up and out!'

When you heard the words you had to be outside already. You got bread, ate it or stuffed it under your shirt. Then you went to the bathroom. Whoever stayed in bed a bit longer didn't get anything done. I can say that I always washed myself.

We were supposed to wash, but in that much of a hurry it was hardly possible. Nevertheless, we did wash a little bit. The water ran. You were not allowed to drink it in Ellrich either, because of the danger of typhoid. But everybody drank.

I had some standing with kapo Keutmann. We were about thirty, thirty-five men. With us in the command there was my

92

uncle Florian, the father of Oscar, and also Russians, Sergei and Micha. Sergei was a foreman like my uncle.

All of these Russians should normally have been in a prisoner-of-war camp. But they were with us in the KZ. Because of this I acquired a bit of Russian.

Jews also worked with us, among others Mr Meier, a small man.[33] It was cold. You had to work hard so that you got into the ground quickly. It was warmer there.

'Meier, come on, get with it,' I said, 'work so that you get in into the ground!'

'Am I crazy? Am I crazy? I don't want to work', he said. 'You shouldn't work with the hands, you should work with the eyes.'

I said:

'Yes, sure, but then you freeze and you are cold.'

But he did not care about that. He preferred to shiver. He did not want to do anything good for those people. But I did it for my own sake, so that I could get into the trench. When you were a little way into the trench, first it was warmer and second, this was the best chance, even in summer, to allow yourself a little rest. If you walked about above, it was always:

'Move, move!'

Nobody was permitted to stand still. If they had caught you standing still, right away you would have got a beating.

When I was finished early I had to help Meier again so that he was finished too and we could slide to the front together. Because of this I had already scolded him several times.

'See, now I am doing your work.'

He answered:

'Why do you work so fast, why?'

I noticed that the soldiers tipped out the hot ashes from their stoves at a certain spot, took a cardboard box, tore off one side in front and waited for the right moment. Then I ran there, quickly, because I dared not let myself be caught, shovelled up the ashes and ran back to my trench. When I had dug so deep that I could no longer be seen from above, that was always an advantage. With the hot ashes you could then warm your hands, and your feet.

Yes, I can tell you that our command included all sorts, from a lawyer to a common labourer. The labourer was tougher, he could stand this. Who the ones with a higher education were, you could tell that right off. They did not know how to hold a shovel. They could not handle one. And because I had not had such an elegant life before, but a life of frugality and hunger, the ill-treatment did not bother me as much as it did a professor, who was now also stuck in prison dress.

If you said something to these once elegant people they reacted quietly and gently. But this did not go down so well in a prison camp. There, if you do not have the appropriate position, you have to howl with the wolves, there you have to work along. But they simply could not do that. They were so highly sensitive, and then mostly went under. If they did not work, they were beaten. Now I'm sure you can imagine: first the beating hurts, and on top of that this: I am a teacher and here I am being beaten by such a common soldier, or by a common foreman.

The soldiers beat you real bad, yes, but I have to say that the prisoners did more of the beating. Whoever had any authority did even more beating than the soldiers.

I had a special shovel that I had selected for myself. It balanced well in the hand. It did not have a big, but a small

94

blade. This was more comfortable for digging and shovelling. It's better to shovel twice, but lighter loads. After work I hid it and shoved it underneath something so that I got it back. Because when they said get your working tools everybody ran off and took what was there. Some didn't care what they got, but I did care. With this shovel digging was almost fun. With it you could nicely cut the white gravelly ground. The kapo and the chief foreman set great store by a nice smooth cut. Down to eighty centimetres in depth you did not have to shore up the sides, but if you went deeper and the sides were not smooth and you then put in cross-beams, then the excavations collapsed. Therefore the kapo wanted everything to be pretty exact. It made me glad too when the trench was nice and straight. Man, neat.

For a time I no longer had any shoes. I took cardboard, stuck red blasting wire through and wrapped it around my feet.[34]

Meier had a second pair of clogs, but he wanted bread and sausage and butter for them. I said:

'Yes, yes, of course. But not right now. I don't have any right now.'

When I saw that he took the clogs along to work I thought to myself: man that won't do. If the block senior sees that, or the kapo or the foreman, he will take them away from him and then he will get a beating!

Then one day at work when I went to get my shovel from its hiding-place, I saw tracks in the snow which led off from the hut in which the tools were kept. I followed them, found the shoes, stuffed them under my jacket, and gave them to my uncle Julius. He gave me his in exchange. They were not worth much any more but I fixed them with wire and cardboard. I never let go, I always tried to make the best out of everything.

Meier came to me right away:

'You stole my shoes!'

'How can you say something like that? I don't even know where your shoes are.'

'I saw tracks, they were your feet.'

'That wasn't me, that must have been somebody else.'

Well anyway, he never got them back.

What became of him I do not know. I do not know whether he would have been glad to see me again.

One time a hydrant had to be turned on. The winter of 1944/1945 was ice-cold.

'Who will do that?'

Otto volunteered again. I climbed down the iron rungs into the deep rectangular shaft, broke the ice away and cleared the hydrant. In between, I climbed up time and again, stomped about to get warm, and then climbed down again. The turning on, I believe, we then did together. The foreman put on the wrench. He was a huge fellow. And then the water came.

I got a chit for one mark or one mark fifty. One mark fifty was the most. For that, in camp, you could get sauerkraut or tobacco.

When we laid a section of pipe, eight or ten men took hold. In our group there was one of those stocky men from East or West Prussia.

'Me. Stand off there.'

Then he took hold all by himself. A length of pipe like that! He lifted it. We, of course, were not able to do that.

Otto (front) with (left to right) his brothers
Waldemar and Max, mother Luise Herzberg
and sister Therese.

Otto's father, Hermann Herzberg.

Cousins Oscar (right) and Bodo.

Otto and his sister Therese (on his left).

Berlin Marzahn, 1936.

Berlin Marzahn, 1936.

Berlin Marzahn, 1936.

Otto's grandmother Charlotte R. with her
sister and brother. Marzahn, after 1937.

Uncle Albert R. (in the cap), Aunt Camba (left),
and in the middle, Otto's sister Therese (white
dress). Marzahn, after 1937.

Therese and Aunt Camba Franzen.

Otto's brother Max. The photo was on his army pass, on his call-up on 6 August 1940 in Berlin Rummelsburg.

Max, 1940.

Kalutschabu (left) and Barono. Otto's
grandmother Charlotte R. stayed with
them in Auschwitz-Birkenau.

Otto's siblings from his mother's
second marriage. They died in
Auschwitz-Birkenau.

1936-37

meine
Schwestern
Traubela
Buchela
Reibkuchen

②

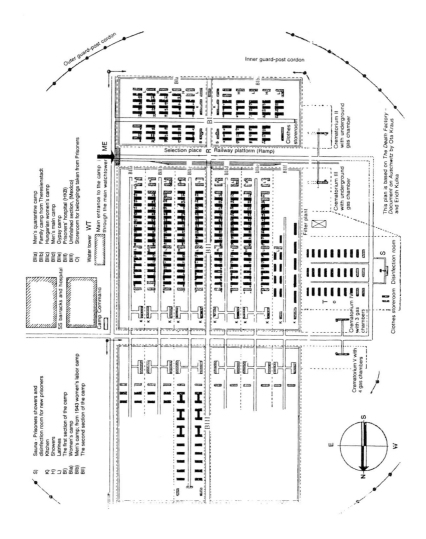

Plan of Auschwitz-Birkenau
concentration camp.

Aerial view taken by the US Air Force.
The sauna, where Otto R. worked, was
in the barracks marked with a cross.

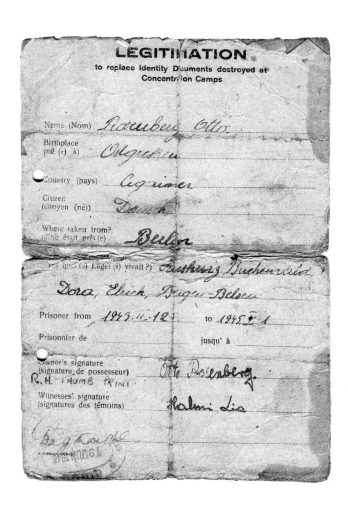

Otto's temporary Identity
Card, Salzwedel.

Otto's mother Luise Herzberg
with his uncle Florian R. 1945.

A victim of Fascism: Otto's
Identity Card.

I observed, in all the time in the KZ, that the Russians were the people who stuck together best. The Sinti did not, nor the Roma, nor the Jews, nor the others, not even the French.

But with the Russians I always found: they really stuck together! When we were loaded into the cars in camp, then they were hardly inside before they would bunch up together tight and start singing their freedom songs. And then our soldiers or SS came and started clubbing with their rifle butts so that the dust really flew. But the Russians did not quit. When one of them went down they dragged him up again and kept right on singing until the army and the SS had had enough, so that they said:

'Let them go.'

The Russians had real fat faces. All the others were emaciated, but they were real big and fat. I wondered about this, and then I observed that they were always putting something into their mouth. They were always eating something, like squirrels, such triangular kernels. I went closer and asked:

'What is that? Give me one.'

They were beechnuts. And do you know what? I ate them the whole time when I was working outside. I had both pockets full. That gives you strength, they are full of pure oil.

Before everything else I always took care that I was clean. In camp we slept on paper sacks that were stuffed with wood-wool.[35] They were full of lice, full of fleas, full of bedbugs. When I was at work, I took my things off. We always built a fire outside. You see there were things I had to burn. There I held my things over the fire and turned them. Then the bedbugs and all those things let themselves fall, because of the heat. In this way I came back to the camp almost clean.

Out there there was also a little rivulet where I washed myself, at noon, as soon as I had a bit of time. In the bathroom you had to be quick. If you did not wash quick enough the others were already shoving. They were getting hit from behind, so they shoved those in front of them out. I was actually very flexible, very quick. And I was not very big. When the SS began beating from above I was never hit, always the others. Furthermore, I also made myself a little bit smaller, well let me tell you, that helped a lot.

In Ellrich it was the only time I got to know an SS man. Well, getting to know him is saying a bit too much.

He said something and I answered him.

And then he said:

'Where did you learn German?'

He was probably not used to that.

'Well,' I said, 'I am from Berlin.'

He came closer and said:

'So, and from what part?'

I described it to him but he probably did not know enough about it. Well, fine. In any event, we went on working, and he continued to walk up and down. Then I found a wrapped piece of bread next to me in the ditch. I did not know exactly: was it from him or not. Then he once threw a long cigarette butt in to me. I took a drag. I turned all wobbly. I thought, now I'm going to drop. You see I didn't smoke, I just took a try.

And then they needed somebody. The SS people on the hill had dogs, and the man responsible had dropped out. The SS man had most likely spoken to the kapo, whether he could spare me. Just over noon, to feed the dogs.

The kapo called me from the trench and took me to the SS man. I called off my number and:

'Present!'

'The dogs need fresh water, the dogs need their lunch. There are dog-biscuits and for each meal they each need one biscuit, sometimes two.'

'Jawoll! All shall be done.'

The first day nothing could be done. The SS guard went along all the time and watched carefully. But I probably did the job satisfactorily. So then he no longer paid me so much attention.

Always when I slid the food in to the dogs, thick slices of chasseur sausage and chunks of meat, I thought:

'If only we would get something like that!'

The SS guard was gone, and the dogs were so stuffed they didn't eat at all.

I took my mess tin, put the food into it and stuck it back under my shirt. Later on, back in the trench – it was not far to our place of work – I took care of my people. But first of all I ate myself.

Dog-biscuit tastes like nut, you know. In all my life I never ate better dog-biscuit then there. You laugh, but that is the way it is.

I do not know how long I was seconded to this duty, but I ate until I had such a fat face. So in other words, again a new boost for survival...

At the 'gawabau' we had a civilian chief foreman. He took us along to his house a few times, two or three men from our detachment. An SS guard went along. There we laid drains. I got a glass of milk there from the woman, or the maid. I was not permitted to accept anything from them, and they were not even allowed to speak to us. I was working directly under the window and just looked in like this. Then she put the milk down for me. I just continued working at first, then I took it. That was as if the sky made the great big sun to shine and it was raining May rain – that is what it was like, such joy. Oh yes, there are still good people!

During the time I worked at Woffleben I saw three men being hanged.

Like so often, we marched from Ellrich to the station. There we got in the cars and rode to Woffleben. We then marched another bit, and then we went to the assembly area.

To the right were the shafts where they were working on the V2. Everything was closed off, with dogs and machine-guns. There were also many towers there.

That is where they hanged the three of them, and all because of a little drive-belt.

The conveyer belts had a motor, and it had a short drive-belt. About forty by forty centimetres.

The drive-belt the whole thing was about, was worn to pieces, it was broken, it had already been replaced. They had taken such a discarded drive-belt, cut it in pieces and nailed it under their clogs, so that they would last longer.

They were given short shrift. A sort of carpet-cleaning rod, a bar with two supports, was put up on the Woffleben grounds. There were, I believe, rings screwed to the rod.

Soldiers marched in. These were not SS men, they were air force ground troops. They had a seagull on their uniform. Some had yellow tabs, some red tabs, and on these tabs there was a seagull – later they were given the grey *Oberschar-* and *Unterscharführer* uniforms by the SS. And one of these soldiers read out loud from a piece of paper:

'For sabotage...'

That made me remember that I too had been convicted of 'sabotage'.

'... have ... themselves of the property of the German nation...'

And so forth. Such a litany they recited.

We all had to assemble around the gallows. Work was interrupted everywhere. SS with dogs and machine-guns and guards, additional guards they set up, watched everything from above. And so the three of them were sentenced to death according to martial law, with immediate effect. They made them stand on a box, three men, a Pole, a Russian, and a Sinto, or Roma – I can't say exactly.

In any case, they had a piece of wood in their mouth, tied behind the head with red blasting wire, and their hands tied at the back, also with blasting wire.

And after the soldier had read the verdict, the boxes were simply pulled away and then they hung there. The hangman was one of the camp kapos. The rumour was that if he hanged the three of them then he was free, that he could go home. He hanged all three of them.

They jerked about for a bit, then it was over.

Then we had to march past the dead, rank by rank in order, the kapo in front, and to look up at them. Anybody who did

* Translator's note: rank specific to the SS. Equates to sergeant and first sergeant in the army.

101

not take a good look was pulled out and thrown against the corpses. And in this manner we marched past the dead.

Later they were cut down. When I was working near by later, while walking about I saw the gags lying there, the pieces of wood, the wire. I picked them up and put them in my pocket. I no longer recall whether it was all three, but I thought:

There, you now have some proof.[36]

For days and weeks I carried these gags in my pocket.

As I have already said: in the evening we rode home in the train, and in the morning to work.

One among us was an older man with his son. I had been sick and had not been able to eat my potatoes. When I was now peeling them he wanted a potato from me. But I didn't give him any. You see, all of us had got the same.

But he took the peelings. Then I heard him say to his son – my uncle heard it too:

'Alas, my boy, we are never going to get out of here anyhow. Do you know what? We will take our own lives. We will go under the train.'

The boy said:

'Oh no.'

He did not want that after all.

In the morning we rode to work and were no longer thinking about this episode. Me and Otto Schmelzer, who is now dead, had heard that something had happened with the train.

Kapo Katschka came towards us.

'You and you, both of you come along. Take a stretcher with you.'

102

This was a cement bin in which you mixed cement.

There were four of us: we, the kapo, and an SS guard.

Now we heard that one of our detachment had jumped under the train.

It is so strange that these things always had to happen to me.

We walked along the tracks and then we found him, here a piece, there a piece, there another piece. We now had to put all that in the bin. I said to Otto Schmelzer:

'Do you know what? This probably happened because I didn't give him a potato.'

Anyway, that is the way I felt about it.

And I thought:

'If I had known that, I would have given him a potato. But now it's too late.'

Now the boy was alone. Later on he lived in Hamburg. I heard from him, and I also went to see him.

But we did not talk about it. It was all still too fresh.

Even now I could not just tell it like this if it were not so many years ago. In the beginning I had to take a break after every third word. That is how much it moved me. I was not able to tell anything about my parents or my brothers and sisters. That was not possible at all.

When holidays came I either sat in a corner, or I cried, or drank, and then it became even worse. That is only better now, only now is it any better. Now you can talk about it better. Even though that will never pass anyway. I have some photographs, there I always light candles.

That is the only consolation you still have: to remember your people.

How what the SS and – as they say – Germans like you or me did was possible at all boggles the mind. That is something nobody can understand. Nobody knows why people can be like that. Even if I have been given an order, I do not have to execute it, not that blatantly. If I have an order, I can let somebody off occasionally. And I think there were very many German soldiers who were also good. But most of them were bad. Most of them were bad. Previously, whenever I had seen our soldiers, in the bus or in the train, I had always looked up to them.

When I recall Marzahn... Near to where we were there were soldiers, there was flak stationed there. When air raids came they shot and somehow I found that interesting. There was nothing threatening about them for me. I even ate lunch with them. They had nothing against me, even though they knew that I was a Sinto, that I came from that place. There was nothing there. But I had to learn bitterly how bad people were.

In Ellrich people were locked into a bunker where you had to stand when they had done something. When it was unlocked again most of them fell out dead. A few also survived.

The corpses always lay between Ellrich and the scheduling office where my cousin worked. I often went to see him. From time to time he helped me, with bread or some soup. He is now dead too.

That was where the corpses were laid out.

And then the following happened: the testicles were always gone, the sex organs. Nobody had an explanation for that.

From then on the corpses were kept under watch. And the person concerned was caught.

It had been a Russian. He had cut off the testicles and eaten them.

We had to fall out on the camp parade ground and stand to. The commander said:

'This man has eaten from these corpses.'

And that this would cause a sickness to come over us, and that the whole camp could become contaminated.

The Russian had to prove that he had really done it. He was stood up on a platform, and there he took these parts, there he took these parts, only with salt – there he ate that up.

The commander said, wisely:

'I would like to judge him, but I do not judge him. I turn him over to his fellow prisoners.'

His fellow prisoners were also Russians, see. And hardly had the commander finished saying this when the Russians had already dragged the man off the platform and seized him and shouted with hollow voices.

They threw him up in the air and stepped apart so that he fell to the ground, threw him up again, and did this several times until he was dead.

Yes, he demonstrated this. On the parade ground he showed it. He ate these parts of the corpses he had cut out, in front of everybody. Yes, he did that.

Otto Rose was there, and he is still alive.

But why this Russian did that, whether from sheer hunger, whether from sheer desperation – maybe he had even gone mad – one does not know.

Once low-flying aircraft came to Woffleben. The word went out: they were the English or the Canadians.

'Oh man, maybe they are coming to liberate us.'

We waved and even tossed up our caps. Suddenly the aircraft came back, came in a dive. I threw myself behind a wagon, some here, others there. Into the dirt, into the mud. Then it turned out they were Stukas who flew right at us and shot at us with machine-guns.

Even though it was rumoured that the Russians were coming ever closer, the camp commander came round one morning and said on the parade ground:

'Whoever volunteers for the SS will be given his freedom, a uniform, and enough to eat.'

You get a bit of training, you have to fight.

Young and inexperienced as I was I thought:

You'd better volunteer! That way you will at least get out of here and will have a weapon in your hand. Then you can at least defend yourself.

I was all set to step forward. But my uncle – he has been dead for a long time now, may God rest him – grabbed me by the collar, slapped me and said:

'Boy, are you mad? Now when the Russians are almost here, when everything is coming to an end, how do you figure you can volunteer?'

Fine, so I stepped back into line.

Many volunteered for the Dirlewangers.[37] That is what they called it. Among others also Ernst Ewald, a cousin of my mother. He then went into Russian captivity. That is the way fate plays it: they put you in a concentration camp, you volunteer, and then you land in a Russian prison camp...

We could already hear the Russians shooting. So we thought: our liberation is approaching, now we will get out.

But we did not get out, on the contrary, they put us in cattle trucks.

We were made to ride back and forth, I do not know for how long. You see, they did nor know where to put us. None of the camps wanted to take us. That they didn't just blow us up was a miracle.

We were, I believe, in those trucks for several weeks: my uncle Florian, my uncle Julius, and the cousin who had worked in the scheduling office. We kept stopping all the time.

There were no toilets in the trucks. There was nothing in there except straw. Sometimes fresh straw came, but you could hardly stand it. Many people died there! Was that ever a stink and a filth! Nobody was permitted to leave the train. Whoever moved even a short way from the trucks was immediately shot by the guards. Many people were shot.

Once even we climbed out too.

We got off during an air-raid alarm. The guards, those dangerous strong men, threw themselves into the ditch, steel helmets over their heads. Then I too climbed out and crawled under the truck.

And when I saw that other prisoners were running towards the pits which were there in the fields, pits with turnips and red beets, I started running too. The SS shot. To the right and left the people fell, but I was not hit. Maybe they were not aiming at me properly.

I also got myself a turnip or two. I was hardly able to carry anything any longer. Then I ran back, crawled back under the truck and climbed up again.

My two uncles helped me too. Oh and were they glad that I was back!

'Here, I have brought you something.'

And then they first ate the beets. We shared, we ate. What was left they then traded for tobacco, and then smoked. I do not smoke, I do not need any tobacco. They puffed away. Yes, I am laughing, but it was all so terribly, terribly serious.

Actually I was already at the end of my tether. When I lifted my arm up I could see that it was only bone, a bone covered by skin.

Once, while we were standing still, I saw a piece of wax paper with smoked herring bones in it lying next to the track. Heaven only knows how long they had already been lying in the sun. I wanted to eat them quickly, but my cousin took them away from me and threw them out.

We were already no longer human beings. More like animals. We were fourteen men and were given one loaf of bread. What is that actually? That is one small slice like this! And one spoonful of tinned meat.

In the end we walked for a bit. There these brave men also shot a lot of people, there I saw what bad people they were.

IX

When we arrived at Bergen-Belsen we were quartered in large
stone houses.[38] These were former army barracks. The rest was
business as usual, room duty and so forth.

I have to admit, I was finished. Only skin and bones. We
searched for potato peels with a stick behind the kitchen and
fried them in the fire even though they were already blue with
rot. That was no longer of any importance. When you found a
bone, who knows from whom, from a dog or some other
animal, you broke it open and sucked it clean, just so that you
had a little bit of taste.

Then suddenly the rumour was that each of us was to get a
big tin of meat, which was unthinkable. The SS condescended
to do this:

'Everybody will get a tin of meat.'

They did not have any bread, but they would try to
organize some bread. Then we thought:

Oh, now the good times are coming.

Then the SS ran away, and overnight the Hungarians were
there. They then guarded us. But they hardly paid any attention to us. Everybody just went where they pleased.

An SS man was lynched in the camp street. However, that
was done by those of us who still had the strength to do it.

I did not see this directly, but I heard the shouting. It happened directly next to my block. An SS man had his pistol stolen and there was a riot. The Allied troops were approaching, and then the last guards also made off.[39]

Whoever was able to sought his freedom. My uncle Julius too.

'We are not going to stay any longer, we are going.'

But I could not walk. My left foot was suppurating and it hurt. The clogs had chafed it. The ankle was totally swollen. The pus ran out. Furthermore my uncle, and those who were with him, wanted to cross some water. I assume it was the river Elbe. And swimming was something I had never learned. So they could not take me with them. I would also only have been an obstruction if we had to run.

What was more, I was still afraid that I would make a mistake.

The houses in which we lay were already empty. I was delirious.

I no longer knew what the game was. My senses had suffered so much that I could no longer find my way.

To go out on the camp street was a sure sentence of death. Despite this I left our block. I went down the camp street and into another block. There I climbed up the stairs all the way to the attic, and in this attic I found a horse, a hobby-horse, and this hobby-horse – I was weak and ill – I dragged down the many steps and went back along the camp street with it to our block, to my room, set it down before my box and laid down again. Yes. And then I had it with me, that hobby-horse. There was nobody left to give orders, see, nobody who said anything.

And then the Allied troops came into the camp, and with this came liberation. But I did not know whose troops these were.

English or American or Russian? All I knew were the German troops. Those I knew. And the Allies confiscated everything.

We were not permitted to take any of the meat tins after all. They said they were poisoned. We were angry when they took the tins away from us. You see, we did not know what really was the matter with them. But then they gave us some dried bread or crispbread and cooked us some chocolate soup or something like that.

I was just as much afraid of the Americans and the English and the Russians as of the German troops, of the SS. You see I had never had any dealings with these people. I did not know: did they intend us evil, or did they intend us good? I was still too young to really grasp all that correctly.

And then I set off after all. We went off together, my uncle Florian, my cousin Willi, and another man whose name I no longer recall. I went and joined them.

We still wore our prisoner's dress and wooden clogs, and the fear was still in our bones. You never knew. There was shooting everywhere. Here a machine-gun chattered, over there somebody fired a shot. You were therefore not safe.

We set off in the direction of the Lüneburg Heath. On a little bridge over some water two armed men came towards us, in short tunics, with caps. Today I know they were Englishmen. But I did not know this then.

They came up to us. And then they said:

'Line up on the bridge!'

They spoke English. They made us line up next to each other along the railing of the bridge.

Now we thought, no good can come of this, now we are really in for it.

111

'Why, we have not done anything.'

We did not understand them, and they could not understand us.

And then I thought:

'Dear God, now I have survived all this time, the tortures and all the deprivations, and you have got over all the hurdles – and now they come and shoot you!'

But we let them line us up, the indifference was still with us. We did not defend ourselves. None of us said no, or even asked why.

And then one of them unslung his machine pistol. The English had these little things that looked like a tin toy.

I closed my eyes and waited for the bang, for the end. But nothing happened.

So I carefully peeped and then permitted myself to take a look.

Then he gives his machine pistol to the other one, reaches into his breast pocket, takes out a little camera and takes our picture!

I think I actually heard the weight that was lifted off me fall to the ground: Wheeew, they are not going to harm us after all!

You simply cannot imagine how that feels when your life is given back to you.

He took our picture and laughed. Then he reached into his pocket once again and pulled out a thin box that had three or four cigarettes in it. And one of these he gave to each of us.

Today I would give almost anything for that photograph.

And after we had then walked on a bit further, I saw a field kitchen up on a ridge, and quite a lot of soldiers. They had stacked their rifles. They were not Germans. In any case I said:

'I am going up there.'

'Come on, man, they will arrest you.'

But I set off anyway and showed these Englishmen or Americans the number on my arm.

They then gave me biscuits and soup, chocolate soup. I ate, and afterwards they gave me a little package, probably their rations. I tucked my jacket into my trousers, tied them tight, and packed everything full.

Then I ran back down the hill. My uncle and the others had already gone a way further on. I whistled. They saw me, stopped, and waited for me.

I said:

'Here, take it!'

You can imagine how fast they ate, with both hands.

You see, it was the first time that we could say: now we can eat as much as we want!

And we were glad, and I heartily joined in for a second time too.

We walked on again for about three kilometres, and then I fell down unconscious.

X

I only came to again in Celle. I was lying in a big room in which beds had been set up and I saw Red Cross nurses.

I was awakened by an alarm clock or some other kind of ringing. I wanted to jump up immediately. You see, I was always fully with it. A bell or something similar meant:

'Out! Out immediately!'

That was a signal for me to be on deck at once, to be ready to go. I wanted to get up immediately. And I still recall that a soothing hand pushed me down again.

'You don't need to be afraid any more. You are free now. It is over. It is over.'

But I could still not really grasp it, that everything was over.

I was given a very little bit to eat, otherwise I would probably have died from it. In this way I was pepped back up very slowly. Like a child. My only desire was food and drink. And this friendliness! The nurses were so loving, so nice! We did not only need food and drink, it was also important to make our spirit well again.

After several weeks I already felt much stronger again. The fear which still breathed down the back of your neck had lessened, the feeling of being murdered and being burned. Now we looked about us. We found:

The danger is over for the time being. We are safe.

I then set off with my cousin Willi.

He disappeared over in Cologne or some place. He never surfaced again.

The acquaintance and my uncle, who is dead now, said:

'Oh, we are not going to Berlin yet. We are staying here.'

I said:

'I have to see whether anybody from my family is still alive, what happened to my brothers and sisters.'

My cousin was of the same mind.

And what made more sense than Berlin? That was our direction.

We marched through the Lüneburg Heath for several days. We slept here and there. But it was very unsafe everywhere. There was much looting going on, and as I have already said, shooting. We did not know where it came from. We saw many people who had armed themselves. But we did not do this.

I recall that we came to a farmhouse and in this farmhouse we asked for food – not as nicely as you normally do this. We demanded it.

There was a woman sitting in the family room with several children. She was weeping terribly.

They had taken everything, and she and her children had nothing left, and the war had not been her fault either. We felt pity for her.

Then she said if we wanted something to eat with the children, if we would be satisfied with what she had, then she would gladly give it to us.

There were only a very few things, but for us they were great: bread, potatoes, soft cheese. We sat down and ate, and we were very satisfied. For us that was a princely meal.

We stayed there for several days, or maybe even one or two weeks. We slept in the house, we ate together with the children, and the woman cooked for us. In other words quite fantastic.

We caught a horse there.

I was walking across a field with my cousin. You see, we didn't spend the whole day indoors. And there a horse came towards us.

'Listen! You go on that side and I'll go on this side.'

We went closer, slowly, in other words carefully – otherwise you see, a horse takes fright and runs away – very gradually, always step by step. He that way, me this way. Talking softly, hand outstretched. Then we had it. You put one hand over its nostrils and grab it by an ear with the other. Then it can no longer get away. We didn't have a rope, see, no line, nothing. When you put your hand over a horse's nostrils it's like putting on a curb bit.

We calmed it down and then took it to the farm. There we stabled it and gave it some feed.

We harnessed the horse to a three-wheeled plough, took turns driving it and ploughed a piece of ground.

We also spoke a lot with the woman and played with the children.

I believe that my experiences on this farm were decisive.

When I arrived there I was full of hate and had the intention to kill. To kill all the people, not only those who had tortured us in the camp.

You did not accept us as Germans, and now that we are getting out, we are going to put you Germans to death too.

We were still far too weak, see, to harm anybody, even though the thought was there. But with time this thought had changed.

I have to remind you that as a child, as a little boy, I had often visited the Christ-the-King-House. For a brief spell I had acted as a server there, and there had even been the intention to make a theologian out of little Otto. Father Petrus, Director Truding, Brother Williges, and all the others, they had seen something like that in me, and I had also been very happy about it, and it would have worked out like that if there had not been any KZ.

And now I recalled my faith again, in connection with this woman and the children. We could have put them to death, see, and nothing would have happened to us. We would just have walked on.

When I left them I had become a different person. Even though I was still not quite normal. A little bit barmy I still was.

When I talk like this, then a fear begins to rise in me. If I had killed somebody, and I can feel this on my skin, I would never have been able to forget that.

We were actually sorry to have to move on. But I said:

'We have to get to Berlin.'

So once again we stomped across the Lüneburg Heath. It was very hot and we came to an inn. There was nobody left in there. Everything was empty. But we found malt beer there, real malt beer. We drank our fill and packed the remaining bottles in a soldier's haversack such as lay in heaps along the roads, together with our bread and a big tin of jam. In the haversack were also the spoons we still had from the KZ, and a knife.

Then we followed a woodland path and hit upon a narrow asphalt road. There we stopped.

One column of lorries after the other drove by us, and among other things an American jeep with a negro who had one of his feet sticking out.

I had a bottle of malt beer in my hand and was just taking a swig, and so I waved at him with the bottle.

Suddenly he put on the brakes, jumped out of the car and ran towards us. Then we both turned around and also began to run.

How frightened we were again at that instant, the both of us!

'Man, what did you do! He is sure to have thought you were threatening him! Now he is coming back and is going to do us in!'

We wanted to run away, but he had such long legs. He caught up to us very quickly.

He tore the bottle from my hand, pulled my head back, took the bottle and held it to my mouth. And then I drank.

When he saw that I drank, he took it away from me again and drained it dry.

'Have you got another one?'

Even though he was speaking English we understood him right away.

Him we would have given everything to. He took them, also drank them empty and threw them away like the first. Then he took us along with him to his car and gave each of us a small package.

When we opened it there were biscuits inside, powdered milk, and also cigarettes. I didn't smoke, you see, and my cousin didn't either. I only learned to smoke on the outside.

Then we crossed the road and went back into the woods, and then we marched and marched.

Suddenly from afar we saw a coach coming towards us. Ho, ho! What a racket! It flew from side to side, the horses were running with sweat. Russians. But not in uniform, former prisoners like us. All drunk. They stopped, got off and came towards us with rifles at the ready.

'Stoj! And: 'Hands up!'

One of them was wearing boxing gloves, real boxing gloves.

'We were in the camp!'

We showed them our numbers.

'Haversacks off!'

We opened the haversacks and they looked inside. They then found the tin of jam.

They had real daggers and with these they cut the tin open. Then they started to spoon away, and then they also shoved a spoonful into each of our mouths.

Then they jumped back on their horses and into the coach. A lightning turn-about, bumm, bumm, and so they galloped away again.

We continued on our way and finally came to the camp at Salzwedel.

That had been an airfield. Now it was an English reception camp.

There we were issued passports, on those they put our thumb prints in red ink.

We also met many former prisoners there, men and women from Hungary, from Romania, from Holland, from all over they came. We again lived in barracks, but our food was much more plentiful. There was enough to eat and drink. We were given brown sugar in linen sacks. I stuffed my pockets full and ate this sugar all the time.

We got to know two Czech women there. One of them was called Pietka.

We wanted to get away from this camp, and so we set off towards Berlin with the two girls. After only a short way we were at odds.

'They are going to get us into a hell of a mess.'

And so we turned back again.

There was a man at Salzwedel who played a wonderful violin. And so we made music.

I got to know a young girl, a Hungarian from Kispest, and her I took along to Berlin.

In Salzwedel we were not free either, you see, even though we were given everything. There we were also registered, if only for the food rations.

We could go where we wanted, but we still ran into prisoners, inmates of the camp. And as long as we kept running into inmates our imprisonment was still not over. More or less, we had all suffered the same sorrows. Maybe some of the girls had even more terrible memories than I had, because they had been raped by the SS or other soldiers.

When you consider that our soldiers, particularly those who had been highly decorated, where you could assume that these were intelligent people you could look up to, sort of, that they were murderers and criminals, who had violated helpless victims!

In any case I went to Berlin with this young Hungarian woman.

When we came to the river Elbe, on one side stood the English, I believe, and on the other the Russians.

There was a temporary bridge. Many cars stood about.

We got aboard a train. The Russians pulled us off again temporarily and interrogated us, but I spoke a little Russian, see. So they let us travel on.

XI

Having arrived in Berlin, the first thing I did was to go to Marzahn. On foot, with a rucksack. But the camp was empty and mostly burned down.

Directly across from Marzahner Platz the farmer's wife had lived whom our teacher had visited so often. But she was no longer there. Frau Schwarz was living there now, the wife of our grocer who had had a store on the lot. She, her husband Walter Schwarz and old mother Schwarz had owned this store. But I only met the daughter and she said:

'The camp was bombed.'

In Marzahn there had been no air-raid bunkers, see, I had already experienced air attacks there. I had visited our flak every day and often been given food there by the soldiers. They had always given me some of their bread and probably had their jokes at my expense, I don't know.

In any case, the daughter Schwarz told me:

'The camp was bombarded with incendiary bombs.'

But she knew that the people who had still lived there had fled into the fields before the attack, just as if they had had a premonition. And that some of them were now living near the Magerviehhof in Friedrichsfelde in some hut or other.

So I searched through the Friedrichsfelde allotment colony.

'Are there gypsies living here?'

Yes, there and there.

In Karlshorst there lived some who had not been in the KZ, and they helped me.

So I found my aunt Camba again with whom I had grown up at my grandmother's. Therefore my relationship with her was very good, and has remained so until the present day.

She was overjoyed, vastly overjoyed.

So I moved into the garden hut with my aunt and my uncle Paul Franzen and their children.

'Come in, boy.'

'My woman?'

'Yes yes, everything OK. Come in.'

Every night I had nightmares. I jumped up, cried and screamed. My aunt thought I was mad.

'Calm down again!'

She had only been in Marzahn, not in Auschwitz or Ravensbrück. Why, I do not know.

And so we lived in Friedrichsfelde, quite a long time. But whether I had registered there I do not recall.

Then my aunt moved away from there, and so did I, to the former front-line soldiers' settlement in Britz.[40] The inhabitants had all been Nazis, and had partly flown the coop or been thrown out. Some of the houses were vacant.

We were put in there. Up there at Grüner Weg. I then lived there with my aunt and her husband and my woman.

The house owner, Mrs Ebert, came to see us. We let her know that we did not want to stay in her house, that she could move back in some time. We could have insisted on our rights, but what for? We did not fancy that anyhow. Most of the people who lived there had the contagion. While they did give us the time of day and talk to us, we still had uneasy feelings.

I registered and was sent to the employment office, already because of the stamp books. And they put me right back to work again! Right after 1945! Work almost like laying pipe in the KZ. It was too hard for me. I was simply not up to it. I said:

'I am not going to do something like that again.'

I was sent to the medical officer. He said:

'No, not under any circumstances. Apply for a certificate as a severely disabled person.'

How quickly they came back to us again! That we were to do such heavy work! The Nazis were still sitting behind the same desks they had always sat behind.[41]

They wanted a birth certificate from me, even though all my documents had been taken away from me!

And in what a tone of voice! We were still intimidated to such an extent that we said, just keep your mouth shut, they are still in control here.

My woman did not understand a word of German. She only spoke her language and Romanes. She was not a Sintezza, but a Roma woman and did not at all fancy staying in Berlin.

We always set off immediately when we heard there was some-body from the KZ, there are still some people alive there, and we searched for them. Most of the time false alarms. In this way I met Poles who had been in Ravensbrück.

I asked them about my mother, about Katza.

And then they said:

'Oh, Katza, yes, we know her.'

'Is she dead or is she still alive?'

'She is alive. She said she was going to Berlin.'

Suddenly I heard that my mother was still alive! Can you imagine what a joy that was?

And I found my mother again.

'My son is still alive!'

'And what about the others?' I asked.

'We have not seen any of them. They are all dead.'

I then also lived with my mother for a time.

My woman, the one I was living with, always wanted to go back to Hungary.

'Németországban azaz nem jó – it is not good to stay here in Germany.'

She was not able to communicate with anybody except me.

'You damnet Nazibanda!'

Those were the only words she could say in German.

She had suffered much, the poor woman.

One day she told me that she wanted to go to Hungary.

We had a man to hand, a German, who spoke fluent Hungarian. He then talked with her and arranged everything with the consulate. There was no stopping her.

My mother also talked with her:

'Girl, stay here.'

My mother was very ill. She had tuberculosis of the lungs, which she had caught in the camp. She then died of the consequences of this disease, see.

I told my woman that I could not go to Hungary with her.

'If something happens I will not be there.'

She packed my camera, my jacket and everything.

'Otto,' she always said to me.

Then I said to her:

'Yes, I will come later.'

I heard nothing from her until my mother died. I lost all contact.

From the front-line soldiers' settlement we went on foraging trips and often stayed away the whole night and the whole day, just to bring home fifty kilos of potatoes, including for my mother and my aunt. I also did business on the black market.

I was often at Alexanderplatz. The Alex, and the Rosenthaler Platz, that was a meeting-place, a trading centre for all sorts of things, for black market and trading deals. You could buy everything there, white bread and dark bread, cigarettes, there was buying and selling, leather jackets, rings. Of course the German police conducted regular raids, drove up, jumped out and took the things away from the people.

There were many discharged soldiers standing about there in their soiled uniforms with crushed caps. I always gave them something, even though I should have said to them:

'Now may the devil spit on you, you dogs!'

But I could not do that. I pitied them so much. One had an arm missing, the next a leg. Sometimes I talked with them.

'Fatherland,' such a one said.

'And don't you get any money?' I asked.

Apparently lots of things had not been taken care of yet.

His wife had left him for another man, she didn't want to even see him again, she wouldn't even let him into the flat.

For God's sake, I thought, what did this man have to suffer, first in the war and now at home.

I said to him:

'I was on the other side. I was in the KZ.'

Yes, some claimed to have heard about the concentration camps, but they claimed never to have had anything to do with them.

'I was at the front.'

If you visit a cemetery it always says on the stones: our good mother, here lies our good father, here lies our good aunt. Where are those who were not good? Just walk about in a cemetery some time and note down: he was good, he was good, and he was also good. They were all good! That makes me wonder too.

Berlin was a pile of rubble. We performed reconstruction work like everybody else. We cleaned stones and laid them on a pile. You did not get very much for doing that.

My friend did not fancy doing that. So they said:

'But Mr Adler, you must put in time at reconstruction like everybody else!'

'You must have taken leave of your senses? What? Here I have just come from the KZ and I am supposed to put in reconstruction time? Did I destroy all this, or somebody else? Why don't they come, the ones who destroyed all this, and reconstruct it?'

But we cleaned stones and removed the rubble. Berlin is our city too. But sometimes it was not easy.

In those days there was no talk yet of compensation or reparation. And when the time came, in the fifties, I had to go all the way to the superior court. They said I was not a true German and had no ties to the city of Berlin.

'Gypsy. Wanderlust. Has no ties to the city of Berlin.'

I was entitled to twenty thousand or thirty thousand

marks. Finally they offered me nine thousand marks out of a hardship fund. However, they wanted to deduct five thousand from this. Welfare that I had received because I had been ill. For my brothers and sisters who died in Birkenau, for my brother Max, for my brother Waldemar who was in the KZ in Bialystok and was killed, for my father who was in the KZ in Bialystok and about whose death I have conflicting reports, and for my mother who died as a result of her imprisonment in a KZ, I did not receive a single penny.

'Prove that this is your mother, that these were your brothers and sisters.'

But I did not have any documents from before! They had taken even my birth certificate away!

I did not even know the names of some of my sisters and brothers from my mother's second marriage. I procured the papers as far as this was possible, and then they said:

'We see a possibility here. You apply for a certificate of inheritance and then you tell us where your mother is buried. Then we must do an exhumation.'

I do not recall what happened next. There was a terrible scene, I tipped the desk over, some people grabbed me.

'You fat pig,' I said. 'You are all Nazis. My mother, who suffered so much, who lost all of her children, you want me to have her exhumed, just so that I can collect this blood money!'

I then renounced all claims, just so that I would not have to be confronted with all this any longer.

And that is what happened to many of us, often because they could not read and could not write and did not know what their rights were.[42]

In those days I went foraging to Eberswalde and to Anger-münde. If the farmers refused to give us anything we waited until evening, went to the storage pits, filled our potato sacks and beat it.

But it was not only for the sake of foraging. They had said: there are many Sinti living there, they are out there in the woods. We stayed overnight with farmers.

For goods we drove to the Müritz and to Röbel. There I went to the mayor and said:

'We are looking for our relatives from the KZ and have to spend the night here. Write out a paper for us that the farmers are to give us something to eat.'

Do you think they gave us anything? You had to go to the neighbours first and talk with them.

'He will not give anything, he has hidden it all.'

And then we went back to the one who had not wanted to give us anything and said:

'You listen here. We have come to you in a decent manner. You are supposed to give us a bit of food so that we can continue on our way. But if you do not do that, then we will report you to the mayor. We know that you have slaughtered a pig, that you have sausage and meat and bacon.'

Then we got something to eat. It was not much, but it was enough.

In Röbel I met a girl I took a fancy to, a Sintezza. But she gave us away and talked. Her mother spoke to me. Now I had to show that I was honest, and because I fancied the girl, I took her. She had also been in Ravensbrück and also in Birkenau. I had not noticed her there. There had been so many people, see, and we had passed each other without looking. Above all I would not have recognized her. In Auschwitz we were all bald. And now she had lovely hair.

We then stayed together for seven years.

At first I stayed with her and her mother in Röbel, in a barracks in the woods. There were also other women of her family living there, and then my aunt from Berlin also came from time to time. The only other man besides myself was her husband, Paul Franzen. So all kinds of women, but no men.

This caused problems with the Russians several times. They always wanted to have our women.

Each time I said:

'Njet, njet, eta tziganka eto moja schena.' No, no, that is my woman.

I was not afraid of the Russians, see. I went at them until the dust flew.

'That is my woman, and that one too!'

And uncle Paul:

'Also my woman, also my woman.'

'All of them your woman?'

'Jawoll, my woman!'

One day one of them came driving up the the lot in a coach. The horses had foam on their mouths and on their necks. He was completely drunk.

He jumped out, went down on his knees, cocked his carbine and laid it on me in order to shoot me. And I believe he would have shot me had he not had a misfire. It just didn't work.

First I stood there paralysed with fear. But then I grasped the situation, ran to the Russian, tore his carbine away, took a stone and knocked the bolt back, put the cartridge in the right way around, cocked the gun and pressed it back into his hands.

'Nu ti bliad ruski.' Now try to shoot!

Then I tore my shirt open.

'Nu stelai ruski. Ja tzigan, ja ne boius.' I am not afraid, I am a gypsy. 'Ti durnoi ili schto?' Are you stupid, or what?

Then he threw the carbine down, came up to me, embraced me and kissed me and cried like a little child.

'Ja nie znal, scho to tzigan!' He hadn't known that I was Sinto!

Then we made friends.

But then he shot into the ceiling and also into the pile of straw, into the big haystack, in which the women had hidden themselves, and I enticed him over to the muck pit. He wore a flashlight at his belt. This I ripped from him, tore the carbine away, gave him a push, and then he fell into the muck pit. Then I ran to the commandatura. There I was questioned, and it did not take long before the 'Mongolians' were there, with a motorcycle with sidecar, two cars, and they grabbed him, and beat him up, and threw him into the sidecar and then drove off with him at full speed.

When I went into Röbel during the following days and passed the commandatura, he came to the cellar window and spoke curses that were so terrible that it is impossible for me to repeat them. But I only laughed. The situation had been saved again, and the Russians no longer came to the lot. Orders from the commandatura:

'They are Sinti. They were in the KZ.'

I had told the commander all that. We then had to dance for him.

'Oh! Charasho!'

We bought a big horse and a covered wagon. This we fixed up, with boards on the sides. And the big horse we sold to a butcher in Berlin.

My mother learned where I was and came:

'Come here, leave this, this is not for you.'

I went back to Berlin and thought about the girl.

'Man. I am simply going to go back there!'

I got dressed, put a note for my mother on the table, and went back to Röbel.

The girl was glad, and her mother too.

We lived in the woods, for real, in a barracks, and I was now next to the fire. My suit was full of holes from the sparks.

My mother came after me and said:

'Mother of God, my boy, just look at you!'

Like it was the custom among the old Sinti next to the fire. That was a different way of life.

But I was a city boy, see, and I had to hear that from my mother-in-law all the time.

I had traded for a particularly lovely horse, a riding horse, Hansi. I shaved his coat short and when I went to hitch him to the wagon he kicked in the whole front. Then my mother-in-law said to her daughter:

'Your city man, he does not know anything!'

On the soft forest floor he had not pulled at all, but as soon as we were on asphalt he began to prance. Such a lovely sight!

But after all he was a riding horse and not a draught horse. When I took the whip and hit him about the ears I thought he was going to kill us all. He jumped about like a rabbit.

Finally my mother said:

'This will not work!'

I took the girl to Berlin with me and she lived with us. She was simple and still very young.

I wanted to take her along on the underground. That was a battle, to get her on the escalator! She had never seen anything like that and she did not want to get on.

She learned quickly and my mother showed her everything. She became as clean and neat as a book.

Because we had noticed that the butchers in Berlin were buying up horses, we drove out time and again, bought horses outside, hitched them to the wagon, drove back into Berlin and sold them. We were able to live well on this until the administration introduced the so-called certificates of destination. From then on the horse was given a stamp on its hoof, and this stamp had to be identical with this certificate or you were not allowed to bring the horse to Berlin. Then it was gone for good.

There were always several of us along and we often met the Russians who were out and about with their panje horses. We did business, and so did they. They always asked:

'Gdje ti rabotajesh?' – Where do you work?

'Artisti.' – We are performers.

'A shto ti delajesh?' – What do you do?

'We sing and dance.'

'Nu dawai!' – Well then, play, sing!

We had guitars. My uncle Paul was a highly talented musician and he began immediately:

'Wichadila na bereg Katiusha...'

That famous Russian song. Then they became enthusiastic and also began to dance along.

On one such occasion one of the Russians wanted to sell me a horse. Whether that had been a white horse or whether it had been the grey I do not recall.

'Vodka jest?'

Did I have vodka. I answered:

'Ja, malo, malo.' A little bit, a little bit.

'Jaja.'

And I bought his horse for a bottle of vodka.

'Charasho.'

I tied the horse on. We mounted and drove on. Maybe three, four kilometres. Suddenly:

'Stoj!'

I said:

'What's the matter now? What does he want?'

'Etot kon eto ne twoi!' – That horse is not yours!

'Who told you that? Net, eto moi kon. A colleague of yours sold it to me. 'Ja kupil na odnu budelku vodki.' – I bought it for a bottle of vodka.

'Ja Kommandant! – I am the commmander!

Then I cursed him in Russian, what kind of a commander he was. And he got excited!

'Ladno', I said. 'Its OK. I am not afraid. Ja tzigan, poni majesh?

Yes, and then everything was not quite the same as before. Well you see, he didn't have anything to drink. So with a bit of humming and hawing I gave him a bottle of vodka too, and then everything was fine again.

I often drank with the Russians, see, vodka po sto grammi, and ate bacon with it. When they were sober they were the best of comrades, but as soon as they were drunk you did not dare say a false word. They immediately went for their guns.

But in those days, because of the KZ, I was not frightened at all. I was not afraid of a pistol, nor of a knife.

I found the Russians agreeable. Today I still find them agreeable. When I hear Russian songs I get all choked up.

Whenever we met them we said:

'Dai mnje Machork.'

Then they gave us machorka and we smoked. My mother too.

The Russians were generous. They wore pigskin trousers and they reached inside and brought out machorka. And when we wanted German newspapers to roll they said:

'Germanskaja gazeta ne charasho, ruskaja gazeta, bumaga charoshaja.' The paper of Russian newspapers is better.

This is the way we drove back and forth all the time until the certificates of destination came. Then that was no longer possible either.

But then also came the break-up between me and my woman. She was unable to have children. What they had done to her in the KZ had been nasty.[43] But because we were not a family there was no cohesion.

My grandmother was dead, my father was dead, my brothers and sisters were dead, there was nobody there anymore. I was all alone and despite my youth had to take all the decisions alone. That was often very hard. Two of my grand-uncles, Anton and Florian, were living in Berlin in the meantime. And that was actually my security.

Then I met my present wife and when she had her first child I went to my two grand-uncles in Wittenau.

'Man you better be careful', they said to me. 'Take a good look at that child. You have to be able to recognize it again. In those hospitals they go and swap the children.'

'For God's sake!'

I called the hospital.

'Hallo, nurse, I wanted to ask you something.'

See, I was not married yet.

'Yes, the baby has arrived. You should be happy, it's a strapping boy.'

I said to my uncles:

'What do you say, I have a son now.'

'You better be careful,' they said. 'You know how it is with those hospitals.'

So I went there in order to visit my son. And speak of the devil, the doctor said to me:

'Please forgive us but there has been a mistake. It is not a son, it is a daughter!'

I was totally confused, I was still so young and inexperienced.

I had found a Brockhaus dictionary in those days by chance. That helped me very much to discover what people were saying, what they were actually talking about. That was very important.

After the birth of my eldest daughter I had another talk with my former woman. We were separating because we had no future.

I said to her:

'Listen, I have a child now.'

She said:

'Come with the baby carriage, bring the child here, I want to see it.'

136

So I brought the child to her. Afterwards she said to me:

'If the child had had your eyes I would have taken it. But it always looks at me with the eyes of that woman. Then I always have to remember that I was in the KZ and that the Germans tortured me. And now I would bring up her children. You belong with the child and no longer with me.'

I then moved with my present wife and our child into my caravan which I had standing in Mainzer Straße. In the winter it was so cold that at night in bed we had to put mittens on the little one. But everything was all right. Later I then found a flat.

With my wife I have seven children today, and some grand-children.

She was always the calming influence in my life. Because the evil others had done to me according to the arbitrary use of power by the Germans, that she made good.

In the beginning it was difficult. Two different worlds met head on, but she was very loving and patient with me and the children, that made the whole matter more easy. In my younger days I went out very often and drank, but came to realize later that that was wrong. See, you only hurt your family.

The KZ number I had made invisible with a tattoo in Hamburg. Now there is an angel covering this disgrace. The number always bothered me. The children kept asking, see, and so I could not find any peace. They wanted to see this number all the time. Now the angel is there, it protects me from all the terrible things that happened then, ever happening again.

I believe that my disagreement with God, yes, afterwards He made it all up to me.

On 8 June 1953 I married my woman. With paeonies, but without a big ado, with potato salad, a little bit to eat and drink.

Notes

1. 'Rosenberg' or 'von Rosenberg' is one of the oldest family names of the Sinti we can trace back to the beginning of the fifteenth century in Germany. A certain Johannes Rosenberg, a Prussian soldier and Tschatschopaskero of the Brandenburg Sinti, was the principal defendant in the trial in 1802 of the so-called 'gypsy conspiracy in Prussia' which ended with an acquittal. Gilsenbach, Reimar: *Tschuttemann Exposé*, 1997; same author: *Oh Django sing deinen Zorn!* (Oh Django sing out your anger), Berlin 1993, p. 65.

2. The establishment of the camp at Berlin-Marzahn, the first racially defined fascist detention camp in Germany, took place without any legal foundation in co-operation between the President of Police of Berlin and the city administration, and with the agreement of the racial-political office of the NSDAP. On 16 June 1936 the Berlin *Lokal-Anzeiger* reported: 'Berlin free of Gypsies'. Hohmann: *Verfolgte ohne Heimat* (Oppressed without a country), p. 70 and Gilsenbach, *Oh Django*, p. 142.

Even Gerhard Stein, the 'alte Kämpfer' ('old fighter', title of honour given to Nazis who had been with Hitler before his putsch attempt in 1923) who investigated the Marzahn camp at some date before 26 October 1936 at the request of the

President of Police of Berlin, who believed that until 1918 the gypsies had had a king, and who said of the 'gypsy bastard' that he was 'the most foul and inferior human being one can imagine, brutal and quarrelsome, work-shy and mendacious, dishonest and dirty, and prone to drunkenness, politically naturally more than unsound, doing naught except inciting his surroundings', could not avoid the conclusion that the forced resettlement had deprived the inmates of their vocations and left them without income. Furthermore he noted: 'The place is in the immediate vicinity of fields irrigated by sewage that wafts foul fumes across, particularly in the evening and under certain weather conditions, which are sometimes insupportable. The water in the newly drilled wells is in fact undrinkable, despite the investigation conducted, so that the people mostly fetch their water from the neighbouring village. By far the worst are the toilet facilities, completely insufficient for such a large number of people. I am convinced that many an illness is being transmitted there.' Federal Archives, Subsidiary Office Berlin-Lichterfelde, Zsg 142, appendix 29.

3. In November 1936 the 'Racial-hygienic and Genetic Research Office of the Reichs Health Authority' began work in Berlin-Dahlem under its director Dr Robert Ritter. Ritter created an important precondition for the holocaust of the Sinti and Roma by assuming that 'gypsy half-breeds', as opposed to 'racially pure gypsies', possessed 'inferior genes', and branding them as being 'highly unstable, unprincipled, unpredictable, undependable, as well as lethargic or restless and irritable', as 'work-shy and asocial'. Reemtsma, Karin, *Sinti*

140

und Roma. Geschichte, Kultur, Gegenwart (Sinti and Roma. History, Culture, Present), Munich 1996, p. 103 et seq.

A 42-page 'genealogy' of the Hamburg and Berlin branches of the Rosenberg family that he drafted, which Eva Justin then probably worked out in detail, demonstrates his methods. We find the great-grandparents of Otto R. merely listed as 'Tschamperdis Freiwald' and 'Reina Klemens'. The alleged 'genealogy' served only to record the complete family for the purpose of condemning them to annihilation. Federal Archives, Subsidiary Office Berlin-Lichterfelde, R 165/160-120.

By March 1942 Ritter and his assistant had recorded 21,498 'gypsies and gypsy half-breeds'. Their 'genealogies' and 'expert comments' were the foundation for the almost complete extermination of these people. See Reemtsma, op. cit., p. 105.

4. According to the Reichs Minister of the Interior's guidelines of 4 April 1938 to the 'asocial persons' decree', 'vagrants (gypsies)' were classed as being asocial, even if they had sufficient income and had no previous convictions. Sending the men from Marzahn to the Sachsenhausen concentration camp was part of a more encompassing wave of arrests. Gilsenbach, *Oh Django*, p. 90.

5. According to Wilhelm Stuckart and Hans Globke: *Commentary to the German Racial Laws*, vol. I, Berlin 1936, 'Jews and gypsies' had 'blood foreign to the species'. The 'First Regulations for the Implementation of the Law for the Protection of the Blood of 14 November 1935' had deprived 'gypsies' of their German citizenship and prohibited marriages. Ibid, p. 88 et seq.

141

6. Control of the camp at Berlin-Marzahn and various other 'gypsy community camps' was being exercised by the Criminal Police. In 1936 the 'Reichs Central Office for the Combat Against Gypsies' had been formed within the 'Reichs Criminal Police Office', to which the newly created 'Offices for Matters Pertaining to Gypsies' within the local control offices of the criminal police reported. Ibid, p. 89.

Among other things, their job was 'to ensure that gypsies did not use trams, did not keep pets, did not visit inns, did not have sexual intercourse with "people of German blood", did not receive mail via post restante. Ibid, p. 107.

7. Leo Karsten was the head of the Berlin 'Office for Matters Pertaining to Gypsies'. His card file and a small fragment of his records are being kept in the Potsdam State Archives under number Pr.Br.Rep.30 Berlin C Tit 198a 3. Zigeuner.

8. Otto R.'s grandmother Charlotte R. appeared in Leni Riefenstahl's film *Tiefland* as an extra. As the film-maker Nina Gladitz revealed in her 1982 film *Zeit des Schweigens und der Dunkelheit* (*Time of Silence and of Darkness*), in 1941 and 1942 Riefenstahl had selected a number of Sinti from the concentration camp of Maxglan near Salzburg. During the shooting of the film the extras were under police guard. The extras from Maxglan were not paid directly (see verdict of 25 June 1985 by the Landgericht Freiburg/Br.). In her court case against the film-maker Riefenstahl presented a set of accounts from which could be seen that from 27 April 1942 onwards Sinti from the camp at Berlin-Marzahn had also been employed for *Tiefland*. 'On 6 April 1943 the "Riefen-

stahl-Film GmbH" paid 3060.45 marks as a 15% "social security compensation payment" for 68 "gypsies" from the Marzahn camp. Virtually all of the Sinti who are listed had been shipped to the Auschwitz-Birkenau extermination camp in early March 1943, in other words about four weeks before the Riefenstahl payment was made. See: Gilsenbach, *Oh Django*, p. 167. After the war Riefenstahl had won a number of court cases dealing with this matter, during which she described Maxglan as a 'welfare and care camp' and called upon the former camp commander SS Sturmbannführer and Kriminalrat Dr Böhmer as an expert witness, who said in this capacity in 1949: 'Not for a single hour was the camp at Salzburg/Maxglan under SS control, SS guard, or even SS influence. Any contradictory claim I reject in the sharpest manner as being a gross exaggeration of the truth and a despicable lie!' See: Dr jur. Anton Böhmer, expert opinion rendered in a court case of L. Riefenstahl against the publisher Kindler 1949 in Munich, photocopy, Nina Gladitz Filmproduction, Kirchzarten 1985.

9. On 13 March 1942 the Reichs Minister of Labour decreed that the 'special regulations in the area of social law' against the Jews were also to apply to 'gypsies'. See: Gilsenbach, *Oh Django*, p. 90.

10. On 16 December 1942 Himmler gave the order that 'gypsy half-breeds' were to be deported to the KZ Auschwitz (ibid, p. 90). The camp at Berlin-Marzahn was dissolved on 1 March 1943 and almost all of the inmates deported to the gypsy camp at Auschwitz-Birkenau (ibid, p. 179). Only two families

remained in the camp whom Ritter had classed as being 'racially pure Sinti and Lalleri gypsies', and who, according to Himmler's plans, were to be put into a reservation in the Ödenburger district at Lake Neusiedler together with seven other families (ibid, p. 155).

11. 14 April 1943: 'A shipment of gypsies has arrived from the territory of the Reich. Twenty men and boys are given the numbers Z-6071 to Z-6090...' From Czech, Danuta: *Kalendarium der Ereignisse im Konzentrationslager Auschwitz-Birkenau 1939–1945* (*Chronicle of Events in the Concentration Camp Auschwitz-Birkenau 1939–1945*), Reinbek 1989, p. 468.

Entry in the Central Register of the Gypsy Camp: 'sequential number: 6084; reason for imprisonment: Zig. D. R. (Gypsy, German Reich); name: Rosenberg; first name: Otto; date of birth: 28.4.27; place of birth: Stallupöhnen; Arrival date in camp: 14.4.43; remarks: (Birk.) (18.5.43)' From: *Gedenkbuch. Die Sinti und Roma im KZ Auschwitz-Birkenau* (*Commemorative Book. The Sinti and Roma in the KZ Auschwitz-Birkenau*), Munich et. al. 1993, vol. 2.

The Central Register of the Gypsy Camp was preserved due to the bravery of the Polish political prisoners, clerks Tadeusz Joachimovsky and Ireneusz Pietrzyk and their fellow prisoner Henryk Porebsky, who stole it from the camp office in view of the planned destruction of the camp, wrapped it in clothing, hid it in a pail, and in July 1944 buried it between barrack No 31 and the fence to the men's camp BIId. The books were disinterred again on 13 January 1949 in the presence of T. Joachimovsky by members of the Auschwitz National Memorial. Compare op. cit. vol. 1 p. XXXVII.

12. 'Boys they sometimes spared were first used by the Nazis as apprentice masons in the construction of the crematoria at Birkenau. The labour force was called the mason school.' From: Kraus, Ota and Kulka, Erich, *Die Todesfabrik Auschwitz* (*The Death Factory Auschwitz*), Berlin 1991, p. 147 et seq.

13. 26 February 1943: 'Based on the decree of 29 January 1943 of the Reich Central Security Office, the first shipment with gypsies from the German Reich is received in the KZ Auschwitz. Some men, women, and children have arrived. They are quartered in the still uncompleted camp in sector BIIe in Birkenau, which is given the name Gypsy Camp BIIe.' From *Chronicle*, op. cit. p. 423.

14. 'These were horse stable barracks with the type designation OKH-type 260/9, which were originally designed for 52 horses, which in Birkenau, however, had to take in over 400 prisoners.' From *Commemorative Book*, op. cit. p. 371.

15. Entries in the Central Register (men): Florian R. on 13 March 1943 under No 2725, Oscar R. on 19 March 1943 under No 4858; Werner August (Bodo) R. on 19 March 1943 under No 4860; Albert R. on 24 March 1943 under No 4976; Henry R. on 28 March 1943 under No 5455; Anton R. on 24 May 1944 under No 9864. Charlotte R., No 5406, and Therese R., No 5407, were entered in the Central Register (women). The date of reception was not recorded for either of them.

16. On 10 July 1942 the Supreme Command of the Wehrmacht ordered that 'gypsies' and 'gypsy half-breeds'

were to be discharged from the Wehrmacht for 'racial-political' reasons. See: Reemtsma, Karin, op. cit. p. 107. In his memoirs Auschwitz commander Höß writes: 'Many men home on furlough from the front were arrested, who were highly decorated, who had been wounded several times, but whose father or mother or grandfather etc. were gypsies or gypsy half-breeds.' See: *KL Auschwitz in den Augen der SS. Höß Broad Kremer (KZ Auschwitz Through the Eyes of the SS. Höß Broad Kremer)*, Verlag des Staatlichen Auschwitz-Museums 1973, p. 64.

17. 'The punishment block (punishment battalion) was block 2 in the main men's camp BIId, where the Jews were being held and which bordered directly on the "gypsy camp"... The prisoners in this block wore a large black dot in front and in back, those that were suspected of intending to break out a large red circle in addition.' See: Kraus/Kulka, op. cit. p. 91 et seq.

18. On 22 November 1943 SS Untersturmführer Hans Schwarzhuber became First Protective Custody Camp Commander of the men's camp BIId. See: *Chronicle*, op. cit., p. 659.

19. 'Towards the end of 1943 the so-called "sauna" was built, a bath and a disinfection facility for clothing.' See: Tadeusz Szymanski, Danuta Szymanska, Tadeusz nieszko, *Das 'Spital' im Zigeuner-Familienlager in Auschwitz-Birkenau (The 'Infirmary' in the Gypsy Family Camp at Auschwitz-Birkenau)*, Die Auschwitz-Hefte, vol. 1, published by the Hamburg Institute for Social Research, Weinheim and Basle 1987, p. 201.

20. In her book *Auschwitz. A Doctor's Story*, Boston 1995, Lucie Adelsberger, a prisoner who took up her duties as camp doctor in the gypsy camp on 21 May 1943, also recalls this 'well-meaning kapo': 'This man was a politically persecuted German who replied to any friendly word in an even more friendly manner. While water was only doled out sparingly and under blows elsewhere in the camp, he generously let the warm water flow in streams over our bodies.' (p. 86).

21. According to Ritter's genealogy, the name of Otto R.'s mother, Elisabeth (Luise) R., in her second marriage was Freiwald. Her only son from this marriage, Paul Freiwald, born on 26 October 1937 in Viersen, is listed in the Central Register as No 205 under this name and date of birth, but under place of birth: Fursen Rheinland. Veronika Freiwald was registered in the Central Register (women) under No 249, and Rosa Freiwald under No 250. The date of reception in the camp was not entered for either of them. The date of death of Veronika F. is illegible, that of Rosa F. (who was registered as Sophie F.) only partially (2.?.44).

22. 'After Mengele had sent a group suffering from spotted fever to the gas chambers in May 1943 he did not repeat the selection of sick infected with spotted fever. Instead he ordered a "delousing action" in the hospital and in the living barracks. In the hospital these "delousings" were conducted in such a way that the seriously ill were dragged off their cots and set on the "smoke-vent stove", while the blankets and the straw sacks were sent to the "sauna" for disinfection... The delousing actions in the camp more or less followed the same pattern,

147

with the exception that after the disinfection of clothing and bedding the gypsies were forced to take a bath in the "sauna" and were only allowed back into the barracks after the 'delousing action' was over, which sometimes lasted from early morning until the evening.' See: Tadeusz Szymanski et. al., op. cit. p. 203.

23. 'These men and women worked in the buildings (called "Canada" by us) in which the valuables of the newly arrived were stored, which they had had to hand in straight away... The things the Canada commando took represented a valuable enrichment of camp life... See: Adelsberger, op. cit., p. 75. 'And then there was a special detachment, whose special duties had earned it the designation special command... This detachment had the horrible job of working in the crematorium. As far as we were able to discover, these prisoners had to confiscate everything the unfortunates who were immediately sent into the gas had brought with them into the death chambers; clothing as well as any remaining private effects... They sometimes came into our camp to bath... After they had been in this job for one, two, or three months they themselves were sent into the gas to ensure their eternal silence.' See: Adelsberger, op. cit. p. 79.

24. 'We were also not allowed to know that there were crematoria. Our Mama told and taught us what we were to say if the SS men questioned us. Then we were supposed to say: "In this chimney and in this oven that is where our daily bread is made for all of us." But we all knew what was going on.' Stojka, Ceija, *Wir leben im Verborgenen. Erinnerungen einer Rom-Zigeunerin*

(*We Live in Obscurity. Memories of a Rom Gypsy*), published by
Karin Berger, Vienna 1989, p. 27 et seq.

25. Mengele had a room in which to work in the sauna. See:
Tadeusz Szymanski et. al., op. cit., p. 205.

26. *Chronicle*, 25 May 1943: 'The SS camp doctor for the gypsy
camp in Birkenau ordered a confinement to camp, during
which 507 gypsy men with numbers Z-7666 to Z-8178 and
528 gypsy women with numbers Z-8331 to Z-8864 were taken
into the gas chambers. Included were several who were sick
with spotted fever and several hundred who were suspected of
having spotted fever' (p. 503). A comparison of the prisoners'
numbers with the Central Register shows that the people
murdered were mainly Poles, many of them from Bialystok and
Suwalki, and Russians.

27. *Chronicle*, 15 May 1944: 'The decision is taken in the
command post of KL Auschwitz to liquidate the inhabitants of
the gypsy family camp BIIe in Birkenau next day. There are
about 6000 men, women, and children housed in camp BIIe.
The current camp commander of sector BIIe, Paul Bonigut, an
opponent of this decision, secretly passes this information on
to gypsies he trusts, so that they will not let themselves be
taken alive.' 16 May 1944: 'Towards 19 hours a confinement
to camp is announced in family camp BIIe in Birkenau. Cars
drive up outside the camp from which SS men armed with
machine-guns descend and surround the camp. The leader of
the action gives the gypsies the order to leave their living
barracks. Because they have been warned, the gypsies armed

149

with knives, spades, crowbars and rocks do not leave the barracks. The astonished SS men go to the leader of the action in the block leader's room. After a consultation, the signal to retire is given by whistle to the SS guards who have surrounded the barracks. The SS men leave camp BIIe. The first attempt to liquidate the gypsies has failed' (p. 774 et seq.).

28. *Chronicle*, 23 May 1944: '1500 gypsies – men, women, and children – who were selected from the gypsy family camp BIIe in Birkenau after the failed attempt by the SS to liquidate the gypsies, have been quartered in blocks 10 and 11 of the main camp. The selected are to be sent to concentration camps inside the Reich' (p. 781).

Chronicle, 2 August 1944: 'In the afternoon an empty freight train is provided at the railway ramp in Birkenau. From KL Auschwitz 1408 male and female gypsies who have been sorted out of camp BIIe and blocks 10 and 11 of the main camp are brought over. They are to be left alive and are therefore to be sent to other concentration camps. Through the fence those departing take their leave of the gypsies remaining in camp BIIe. Towards 19 hours the train leaves the ramp in Birkenau... The destination of the train is KL Buchenwald' (p. 838).

'After the evening line-up confinement to camp is ordered in KL Auschwitz II, and confinement to block in the gypsy family camp BIIe. Camp BIIe as well as some further barracks in which there are still gypsies are surrounded by armed SS men. Lorries drive into the camp, with which 2897 helpless women, men, and children are driven to the gas chambers in the crematorium. After gassing, the corpses of the murdered are burned in a pit next to the crematorium because the ovens of the crematorium are not working' (p. 838).

29. *Chronicle*, 3 August 1944: 'The shipment of gypsies from KL Auschwitz II, Birkenau, arrives in KL Buchenwald. The shipment consists of 918 gypsies; included among them are 105 boys age nine to fourteen, 393 youths age 15 to 24, 330 men age 25 to 44, 59 men age 45 to 64. Two men are over 65, one man is named without age, five men are not listed. The women are probably sent to a subsidiary camp' (p. 840).

'Out of the total number of 4183 prisoners who were sent to other camps from the gypsy camp... 1800 gypsies must be deducted who were sent back to Auschwitz and were killed in the gas chambers.' See: Thadeusz Szymanski et. al., op. cit., p. 207.

30. After the destruction of the V1 and V2 rocket production facilities in Peenemünde on 17/18 August 1943 by a British air attack, prisoners from Buchenwald were brought to the vicinity of Nordhausen in the southern Harz in lorries during the night of 27/28 August 1943, in order to enlarge an already existing tunnel system under the Kohnstein (mountain). See Pachaly, Erhard and Pelny, Kurt, *KZ Mittelbau-Dora*, Berlin 1990, p. 7 et seq. Objective: construction of a factory with a production capacity of 1800 rockets per month (ibid, p. 65). By December 1943 there were already 10,745 prisoners working in this camp (ibid, p. 68).The daily death toll was roughly 200 prisoners, partly due to mass hangings on the crabs (ibid, p. 72 et seq.). After the first series of V1 launches against English cities in the second half of June 1944 a reduction of the death rate was

recorded. In August 1944 100 prisoners out of 12,000 died (ibid, p. 95). On 28 October 1944 the camp with 15,000 prisoners was constituted as KZ Mittelbau-Dora and made independent of Buchenwald. See: Weinmann, Martin, pub., *Das nationalsozialistische Lagersystem* (*The National Socialist Camp System*), CCP. Zweitausendeins, without place or date, pp. 565 and 739.

'There were large groups of gypsies in KZ Mittelbau-Dora. The statistics record 1185 gypsies for 1 November 1944. On 20 February 1945 there were 365 people in the subsidiary camp Ellrich who wore the black triangle, and on 15 December 1944 there were 479 in the subsidiary camp Harzungen. This data permits the conclusion that there were between 4000 and 5000 gypsies in Dora and its subsidiary commands.' See Pachaly and Pelny, op. cit., p. 111.

31. The subsidiary command Ellrich near Nordhausen belonging to Dora-Mittelbau, was installed on 2 May 1944 under the code name 'Erich'. It had an average of 8000 prisoners. Ibid, p. 569.

32. The construction site in Woffleben was begun under the Himmelsberg as project BIII in 1944/45 (Ibid, p.169). The objective was, among other things, the production of the secret weapons 'typhoon', 'butterfly', and 'lizard'. At the end of September 1944 there were 2660 prisoners working there. 'In view of the intended special activities and special production, the objective was to increase the number of prisoners to about 5320, whereby only a part of these prisoners could be quartered in the prison barracks complex at Woffleben. So the

greater part of these assigned prisoners had to be supplied by the prison camp complex at Ellrich' (ibid, p. 173 et seq.).

33. 'The Jews were assigned the heaviest work ... The SS preferred to order Jews up onto the "terrace", in other words, to work above ground. They dug trenches for the water supply or for the installation of drainage canals. They were also used for the levelling of the terrain or similar work' (ibid, p. 110).

34. From the monthly report of the prisoner's infirmary of work camp Erich of 21 December 1944 to 20 January 1945: 'Due to the poor supply with shoes frostbite of the lower members frequently occurs which is difficult to treat due to lack of bandaging material.' Out of 6975 prisoners, 513 died during this reporting period. See: Pachaly/Pelny, op. cit., p. 252 et seq.

35. From the same: 'Camp Erich is totally louse-ridden. Delousing measures are currently being conducted... Unfortunately complete success cannot be expected, because only 200 bales of wood-wool could be made available and no new wool at all could be supplied for the renewal of the straw sacks.'

36. The witness of an execution in Dora-Mittelbau reports: 'The seven prisoners had a wooden gag put into their mouths, which was tied in back with a wire, so that they could neither call out nor speak' (ibid, p. 99).

37. SS Obersturmführer Oskar Dirlewanger was the commander of an SS probation brigade made up of 'volunteers', primarily KZ prisoners who were Reichs Germans.

38. On 1 January 1945 there were 18,465 people imprisoned at Bergen-Belsen, and on 1 March there were already 41,520 due to the evacuation of concentration camps closer to the front. 'In the month of March the death rate was so unbelievably high (as already underlined, in this month alone 18,168 people died), that the camp population no longer increased to any great extent despite constantly arriving shipments.' See: Kolb, Eberhard, Bergen-Belsen. *Vom 'Aufenthaltslager' zum Konzentrationslager 1943–1945 (Bergen-Belsen. From a 'Residence Camp' to a Concentration Camp 1943–1945)*, Göttingen 1985, p. 40.

The shipments from KZ Dora-Mittelbau arrived during the second week in April. 'Since 4 April this camp with its numerous subsidiary commands was being evacuated ahead of the approaching American troops; an estimated 25,000 to 30,000 Dora prisoners reached Bergen-Belsen in freight cars after a ride lasting several days and interrupted by bomb attacks, detours, and traffic holdups. These shipments, however, were no longer housed in the camp itself but in the barracks of the neighbouring troop training grounds' (ibid, p. 41). The final sentence explains why Otto R. remembers large stone buildings, of which there were none in the prisoners' sector of the actual camp.

39. Himmler had been persuaded not to have the camp evacuated like the other camps near the front, but to hand it over to the British.

'The truce agreement signed during the night of 12/13 April stipulated the neutralization of an area 8 km long and 6 km wide surrounding the Bergen-Belsen camp. It also stipulated that until the camp could be taken over by British troops, the guard would be taken over from the SS by members of the German Wehrmacht (including a unit of Hungarian soldiers), who had been promised free withdrawal to the German lines with their weapons, equipment, and vehicles within six days. As far as the personnel of the SS command was concerned, the wording of the truce agreement was quite vague... In fact, the greater part of the SS people withdrew on 13 April, while Kramer remained behind in Bergen-Belsen with 50 SS men and 30 female supervisors' (ibid, p. 48 et seq.).

'On the day of liberation and during the following night ... wild scenes were enacted ... SS and army guards shot into the crowds and killed many people; a number of hated capos were lynched... The first British medical unit arrived in Bergen-Belsen on 17 April... On 24 April the evacuation of the camp began. Not only the sick, but also the more or less still healthy were now moved to the military barracks on the troop training grounds...' (ibid, p. 50 et. seq.).

Despite greatest efforts to save the survivors, after the liberation a further approximately 13,000 people died. See: *Bergen-Belsen. Texte und Bilder der Ausstellung in der zentralen Gedenkstätte des Landes Niedersachsen auf dem Gelände des ehemaligen Konzentrations- und Kriegsgefangenenlagers Bergen-Belsen (Bergen-Belsen. Text and Illustrations to the Exhibit in the Central Memorial of the State of Lower Saxony on the Grounds of the Former Concentration and Prisoner of War Camp Bergen-Belsen)*, published by the Landerszentrale für politische Bildung, Hannover, Hamelin 1990, p. IV/1.

40. The 'Front Fighter's Settlement "Schlageter"' had been inaugurated on 1 August 1934. See: *Neuköllner Kulturverein e.*

V.: Vom Ilsenhof zum Highdeck. Modelle sozialen Wohnens in Neukölln (Neukölln Cultural Association e. V. From the Ilsenhof to the Highdeck. Models of Social Living in Neukölln), published by Brigitte Jacob and Harald Ramm, Berlin 1987, p. 101.

41. Ritter, who had been promoted to Chief of the Reich Health Office in 1944, was appointed in 1947 as Chief of the Welfare Office for the Emotionally and Nervously Disordered and the Juvenile Psychiatry Service in Frankfurt/Main. Justin, who had come out of her denazification proceedings with the classification 'not involved', was brought in by him in 1948 as a 'criminal psychologist'. All subsequent court cases initiated against them were quashed. See Reemtsma, op. cit., p. 130 et seq. Leo Karsten stayed with the criminal police and moved to Karlsruhe. Ibid, p. 126.

42. Otto Rosenberg only knew the Sinti names of his stepsisters from his mother's second marriage, Traubela, Buchela, and Reibkuchen. He did not have access to the Ritter 'genealogy' in which these names were added in pencil and where with his stepbrother Paul, the civil names Veronika, born 29.10.34, and Rosa, born 26.2.36, are also recorded. Together with all the other 'genealogies' Ritter gave it to Eva Justin, who passed them on in 1949 to an employee of the 'vagrants' centre' at the Bavarian State Criminal Office. After having been used for years, the genealogies came into the possession of professor Hermann Arnold and then of the Anthropological Institute of the University of Mainz. After protests by the 'Association of Endangered Peoples' they were finally confiscated by the Federal Archives in 1981. See: letter

of 13 March 1984 by solicitor Hartmut Wächter to the State Court Munich I.

'For their decisions on the applications for reparations by the victims, the courts drew upon former members of the 'gypsy office' in the Reichs Central Security Office and the 'racial hygienic research office' of the Reichs Health Ministry.' See: Reemtsma, op. cit. p. 133.

According to a verdict by the Federal Supreme Court, 'gypsies' were only victims of persecution on racial grounds from the year 1943 on. This decision was revised in 1963. On 31 December 1969 the deadline for applications by the victims ran out. In 1981 the Federal Government issued new guidelines for the 'compensation of hardships in individual cases for victims of non-Jewish descent'. 'However, only those who had never before applied for reparations were eligible to apply. Those Sinti and Roma whose applications had been rejected under the former body of law had no claim to the already low maximum sum of DM 5000 or to a small pension.' Ibid, p. 134.

43. KZ doctors such as gynaecologist Professor Dr Clauberg developed X-ray and other procedures in order to be able to perform 1000 sterilizations per day. 'They primarily conducted their experiments with 'gypsies' who were imprisoned in KZ Auschwitz-Birkenau. As late as March 1945, only a few weeks before the end of the war, Clausberg still sterilized 20 Sinti girls in the camp at Ravensbrück.' See: Gilsenbach, *Oh Django*, p. 82 et seq.